Crash Course in Children's Services

Crash Course in Children's Services

Penny Peck

Crash Course Series

LIBRARIES

U N L I M I T E D

A Member of the Greenwood Publishing Group

Westport, Connecticut • London

Library of Congress Cataloging-in-Publication Data

Peck, Penny.
   Crash course in children's services / by Penny Peck.
      p. cm. — (Crash course)
   Includes bibliographical references and index.
   ISBN 1-59158-352-7 (pbk : alk. paper)
   1. Children's libraries—United States. I. Title.
Z718.2.U6P43 2006
027.62'5—dc22   2006023646

British Library Cataloguing in Publication Data is available.

Library of Congress Catalog Card Number: 2006023646
ISBN: 1-59158-352-7

First published in 2006

Libraries Unlimited, 88 Post Road West, Westport, CT 06881
A Member of the Greenwood Publishing Group, Inc.
www.lu.com

Printed in the United States of America

The paper used in this book complies with the
Permanent Paper Standard issued by the National
Information Standards Organization (Z39.48–1984).

10   9   8   7   6   5   4   3   2   1

Contents

INTRODUCTION

Welcome to the world of library service to children! Helping children find great books to read, assisting them with homework assignments, and leading them to be lifelong readers and library users is a very rewarding career. But there can always be frustrations, too. Children may be left by inconsiderate parents who expect the library to serve as a babysitter. This Crash Course guide is intended to help you find job satisfaction as well as cope with a variety of different aspects of serving children in your public library.

Designed for persons working in small libraries, this book will increase your comfort level while working with children in your library. This guide covers library services particular to children, such as programming including storytime and book discussion groups.

In many small public libraries, only a part-time person may be assigned to children's services. If no single person is assigned full-time to conduct programs or to offer homework assistance, your volunteers may be as important as volunteers in schools or in a hospital. This book gives lots of practical advice on basic children's library services that you or another staff member can perform with confidence when there is no children's librarian at that site. It will also be very useful for you to train new staff or volunteers to work with children.

This book covers tried and true, practical library service to children based on twenty years' experience in a busy suburban public library, working in a community with no school librarians at the elementary level. It also brings the experience of teaching others who will be working with children.

Because this is a "crash course," meaning a brief, quick handbook on serving children in a library, it cannot cover everything. It will not go into specific service issues to teens or young adults, but some of the advice can easily be adapted to serving that audience. Nor will we cover bulletin boards, making flyers, how to write a press release, or management of employees. Many other books will go into detail on how to perform those tasks; this book covers procedures specific to serving children in the library. It also does not go into circulation or related issues.

So whether you are assigned to the Children's Desk or are responsible for choosing and perhaps training this person, this book is for you. It is not all inclusive. It is also a quick overview for those already on the job who need some assistance in taking on a new task such as storytime or a summer reading program. Alongside the relatively brief descriptions of practices and procedures you will find references to books and Web sites for you to further explore a topic of interest.

What are the essential qualifications of those who work with children in a library? First is the interest in and concern for children and their well-being. Also, children's services is more book driven than some other library services that are currently more centered on using computers for research; helping to nurture the love of reading is still a top priority in children's services. That is why so many of us went into the profession in the first place: to promote books and reading for fun, as well as help children be better students. So if you enjoy books and helping children, you are well on your way to being a successful children's library service provider, and hopefully this book will give you more confidence so you will go on to achieve job satisfaction. After all, what could be more enriching than nurturing the love of books and reading in a child, making that person a lifelong learner?

Chapter 1

Reference

REFERENCE: THE FIRST STEP

Reference is often the first step in assisting children, parents, and teachers who come to the Children's Desk seeking books, materials, and information. Folks come up to the desk and say "I need a book about frogs," and the staff member explores whether this is for a report on frogs, or if the family has a new pet frog, or the student has to dissect a frog. This chapter defines the child as your customer and provides tips on the reference interview, a simple overview of child development levels to show what children can handle at certain ages, and tips for assisting parents or teachers in finding materials. The chapter also covers teaching children how to perform basic card catalog and public access catalog searches and about the different Dewey Decimal Classification sections and fiction sections found in most libraries.

CHILDREN AS REFERENCE CUSTOMERS

When a young person comes into the library, that child deserves the same level of customer service as an adult. Children are in the library to find books and materials for homework as well as recreational reading; in many libraries, circulation of children's materials is greater than that of adult materials. Once you become accustomed to assisting children, you may find that they are a rewarding group to serve; they express excitement at finding what they like as well as being appreciative, and can be regular customers. There are a few things you will benefit from knowing when it comes to serving children in the library, in regard to how they may differ from our adult customers.

Children are not mini adults. When it comes to library reference, children often are more straightforward in their requests than adults are. Adults may ask, "Where are the cookbooks?" but children may be more specific, "I need a recipe for my Native American Indian report on the Navajo tribe." It is possible that this is because children know what the specific assignment is and may even have a handout spelling out what is needed. When adults are asked questions to help figure out what they really need, some get edgy, as if the librarian is invading their privacy. Children seem much less resistant to the librarian's questions; maybe they realize the librarian is asking so he or she can find exactly what students are looking for. So in some ways, children can be easier to wait on than adults at the reference desk, because they are usually more straightforward than adults in the way they ask for things.

Sometimes children will have trouble understanding that a library doesn't own every book ever made, or that a library doesn't have enough books on a topic for every person that asks. Children have less experience in "shopping" than most adults, so they don't always do so efficiently. Many of us have seen children playing on the library computer for an hour, then rushing up to the desk to ask for a book, but they need it right now since their parents are in the parking lot, honking their horns to pick them up. So we have to help them use their time more efficiently. It is okay to tell a child, "Next time, ask for what you need before you sit down at the computer so we don't have to rush to find things." An adult would be offended by such advice, but to children, it is just information that helps you to help them, especially if spoken in a kind voice.

Younger children may be unable to evaluate whether what you find for them is what they want. Don't hesitate to ask follow-up questions after they have looked at the material for a few minutes: "Is that on your reading level, or do you want me to find something easier (or more challenging) to read?" You can also ask if what was found fits the assignment, or if you and the student should keep looking. Students may need to be taught that they can ask for several things at once, rather than come up to the desk every five minutes with a new request. Librarians may be the first people children work with on a regular basis in this type of retail experience, so if we offer advice on the best ways to ask for help, it isn't just to make our jobs easier. It can be advice that helps them in the future when they have interactions with other adults who are helping them, such as doctors or barbers.

Reference assistance to children can include finding materials for homework assignments, as well as finding recreational reading materials. Even with the Internet and other online resources, most children are in the library to find books to borrow. Whether the books sought are for fun or for homework, both requests are equally important when serving children. Often the teacher has given specific instructions on what children are to look for, and we need to help them fulfill that goal with the best customer service possible.

Children do have strong opinions, especially when it comes to recreational reading. They often are open-minded and will try a longer book or something else that is new to them, but when they ask for a Goosebumps book, see if you can find one for them. Don't just assume that it is not literary enough to give them; if that is what they want to read for fun, try to meet that need. You may ask if it is for a book report, check that the teacher will allow a series book for a book report (many do not), and offer alternatives if it is determined that the request won't fit for a school assignment. But to be snobbish about what children read can backfire; children won't find you helpful and will not listen to your advice on what to read in the future.

CHILD DEVELOPMENT

When children are our customers, it can be beneficial to know some basics of child development so we can serve them better. There can be some developmental reasons for children's inability to express their needs or to work efficiently in the library. Knowing a few facts about child development can help us to be better listeners and be more patient with younger customers. Knowing some child development basics can remove the filter between you and the child and make your interactions more effective.

It is often determined that children under the age of eight cannot always tell right from wrong or tell reality from imagination. That is why age eight is referred to as "the age of reason" for children to be able to be on their own. Therefore, many libraries will have a policy that children must be age eight to be in the library without adult supervision. This rule is based on child development principles. Those who work with children will notice that they may have to tell a five-year-old the same rules over and over, but a nine-year-old may remember from one minute to the next that there is a rule against running in the library. If the five-year-olds forget, you will need to remind them every time they come to the library.

Early childhood is often set at ages three to eight, an age group that is usually in the library with a parent or caregiver. This age group takes great pride in accomplishments, so let them help in finding books they request; even if they cannot type, let them watch you use the online catalog. Partner with them to help them find what they are asking for instead of just handing them what they have requested.

Later childhood is usually set at ages nine to twelve, when a child often will go to the library without an adult. Or, if an adult comes with the child to the library, often the child will separate from the adult when it comes time to ask for materials. This age group is very good at concrete problem solving, is industrious, and takes initiative. These children like to use the online computers to find their own materials or may want you to assist, but with them taking the lead.

Adolescents, or teen customers, enjoy making their own decisions. Parents and other adults, like librarians and teachers, can show them the results of their choices and help them choose again for different results if that is what is needed, but teens are trying to separate from childhood and show their independence. They often need time to daydream and may be forgetful, but they will appreciate any adult help that comes across as nonjudgmental.

Brain Development

Recent studies on brain development in babies and very young children have been featured prominently in news magazines and on television. A great deal of pressure is placed on parents to help babies from day one to develop language skills, to be read to, to use their imaginations, to be stimulated visually and with music, and to challenge themselves. That means parents may ask for books on physics for a three-year-old. The librarian can help by offering great picture books, music CDs for children, and CD-ROM learning games that are age appropriate, as well as parenting books. But preschoolers still do not have the fine motor skills needed to keyboard, and parents may need to be helped to learn what their children, even the most advanced, can and cannot be expected to do. Then these parents should be prepared to help their children with tasks that they can, rather than frustrate their children with tasks that they cannot, do. Also, every child who is the same age is not the same developmentally, so a great rule of thumb is to be flexible and let parents determine what books would be the best "fit" for their children.

Children and Their Needs

For more about child development in general, read the studies by Abraham Maslow, Erik Erikson, or Jean Piaget. Basically, each of these authors outlined a hierarchy of needs in childhood. A shorthand way to remember what may fit a child, depending on his or her age, is that children under age six are trying to achieve autonomy, children ages six to nine are developing initiative, those ages nine to twelve are becoming industrious, and teens are establishing their identity. That is one reason preschoolers say "No!" frequently; they are establishing autonomy, and why teens may seem rude (but don't take it personally); they are defining who they are.

Children and Choices

Just like adults, children should be offered choices while in the library. Let them look at books both above and below their grade level and see what they choose. If they're looking for a nonfiction topic, children will often choose books that may be too difficult to read from cover to cover but will serve a need because the photographs are well done. If you provide choices, children are more likely to leave with something; if you only offer one book, there is more of a chance that it won't be desirable and they will leave empty handed.

REFERENCE INTERVIEW WITH CHILDREN

Children's reference is a basic service that can vary from a quick interaction to more involved discussion, depending on the information the person is seeking. If the question is "Where are the joke books?" it can be as easy as pointing to that area of the nonfiction section. If the request involves a student just starting to find information for a research report, it can be more involved. But these interactions, whether they are brief or more complex, usually begin with the reference interview.

The reference interview is basically talking to the person to figure out what he or she wants or needs (which is two different things; more on that in chapter 2). If children ask for joke books, we can talk to them while walking to that Dewey numbered area and find out what grade they are in. If they are first and second graders, we may also want to show them the series of joke books by Lynn Hall, which most libraries catalog in the easy readers, and also show them that section as well as nonfiction. We can talk to them and find out that they really didn't mean joke books, but they want "Garfield" or "Family Circus" paperbacks, which the library may have in the children's paperback section. Or they may have meant humorous books, like Dav Pilkey's Captain Underpants series, which the library has in the fiction section. So even a simple request, which at first sounds like a directional question along the lines of asking, "Where's the restroom?" can benefit from the reference interview.

Commonly Asked Questions

So the interview involves asking questions to help pinpoint what the person wants. Start with

"Is this for you?" (It may be for a sibling who is older or younger than the child.)

"What grade are you in?"

"Is this for a homework assignment?"

If so, "Do you have a handout or something written down about the homework assignment?"

I always ask this last question but also make clear that I can help regardless of the answer. I don't want that child to give up just because he or she forgot to bring the homework paper. If the child has a handout, it just makes handling the request easier because the teacher may have provided more details on the written instructions than the child will remember.

Children often will be direct with what they ask because, hopefully, their teachers have been direct in describing what they are supposed to find for the report. You may even want to know the name of the school and teacher; most fifth graders do the staple state reports, covering history, geography, flag, etc., but you will get one teacher who wants them just to do a poster of the state, showing where one would go on a vacation in that state (then you head for the adult travel books instead of the state report books or *World Book Encyclopedia*). Also, how long is the homework assignment supposed to be, one page or ten? If it is one page on Benjamin Franklin, then the encyclopedia will actually work better than a biography; but a ten-page paper would call for a biography. Do you need pictures? Maps? Children often begin, "I need a book about" when they may only need a paragraph about the subject. In that case, an encyclopedia article may be a better choice.

This recently happened to me: An eighth-grade boy was sure his teacher wanted him to get a book on Felix Whitley. I asked what class it was for (could it be a famous scientist I hadn't heard of?). It was for U.S. history, an assignment on colonial times. Well, I knew I didn't know of a Felix Whitley, and my B.A. is in U.S. history, so I asked, "Are you sure you don't have a handout from the teacher helping us spell the name? When I typed it into our computer, I didn't get anything." He dug in his backpack and a few minutes later had the handout—he wanted a book on Phyllis Wheatley, the colonial African American poet. Eureka! Yes, we had several books on Phyllis Wheatley; the Chelsea House Black Americans of Achievement biography was perfect for his grade/reading level. In a situation like this, you could even make a photocopy of the handout if you think other students will be coming from that same class. Most small and even branch libraries serve a distinct number of schools, so you know you will see students with the same assignment.

"May I help you?" usually gets a "No thanks," or "Just looking." How about "Did you find what you were looking for?" or "Did you need something for a homework assignment?" Those last two questions often get a more accurate response. Walk around the library if possible the way a waitress walks around her tables; don't just wait for children to come up to the counter.

So, keep asking questions until you get some type of result. You are not invading the students' privacy but trying to help them. For children under age ten, often the parent has brought them in and can help us figure out what is needed. For kids ten and up, usually the students have a better idea than the parents, unless the parent was in the classroom! I often engage the child and parent together, not just one or the other. Sometimes that means you have to get the parent to back off a little, but you can do that with humor and kindness. Sometimes just making eye contact with the child will signal the parent to let the child respond. If that doesn't work, ask the child if he or she remembers what the teacher said; that often works since the parent wants to know this, too. Parents often are partners in helping the child do homework, so their participation is important, as long as they don't take over the reference interview.

LIBRARY USE INTRODUCTION

Whether it is one on one, or during a class field trip, people need to be taught how a library is arranged and how to find things. This process changes frequently. Think of your own time in high school using the *Readers' Guide to Periodicals* to find magazine articles; now students can print the entire article using online databases like Infotrac. We "teach" library skills, formally to a class when students are at the library for a tour, and also informally, like when you are showing a student how to look for a book using the online catalog. Many teachable moments come up in the library, and they give us the opportunity to explain the Dewey Decimal Classification System and allow us to demonstrate research skills. One way to take advantage of these teachable moments is to narrate what you are doing while helping someone find a book; a student can watch while you look up a book using the online catalog and get a feeling for how you are using it and what steps you are taking.

Library Tours and Other Times for Giving Instruction

Class tours are opportunities to show what your library has to offer, how it is organized, about library cards, and basic library rules. Much more is presented on this topic in chapter 6, but a key element is helping students be self-sufficient. Sure, anyone will appreciate it when you look up the book and hand it to him or her, but he or she will also appreciate when you demonstrate how you found it. This is like the adage, "Give a man a fish and he eats for a day, teach a man to fish and he eats forever." Showing how to find things in a library will empower a child to be a confident library user now and for a lifetime. This is especially true when you use relevant examples while teaching library skills; if the student needs sources for a country report, use that concrete example when you teach the student how to use the online or card catalog, as well as Internet resources. Other teachable moments can occur when there is something in the news that you can use as an example when helping children in the library. If there recently has been a natural disaster like an earthquake, you can use that as the subject of an online search when showing students how to use the catalog. Or if there is a current hit movie based on a children's book, use that book title as an example of something they can search.

Breakdown by Age

Because online catalogs usually require a student to spell correctly and use the keyboard effectively, most students cannot use the online catalog easily until third grade. They can read at a much higher grade level than they can spell; they can read an entire book on *Tyrannosaurus rex* but cannot spell it. They may not grasp the idea of entering the last name first when searching for an author. So the formal teaching of the online catalog may need to wait until third grade, whereas using an old fashioned card catalog can be done by first and second graders. Some school libraries still have card catalogs, so many children still receive their first library instruction using the card catalog.

TEACHERS AND PARENTS AS CUSTOMERS

In many communities, the public elementary schools have no school librarians. Teachers bring their classes on scheduled tours of the public library, where they would like the children to learn library and research skills. However, this is not the only service we should provide. Another service important to teachers is finding great stories to read out loud to their classes, or books to take to their classes that tie into the curriculum. When teachers need a large number of books for their classes, I encourage then to phone ahead and let me know what they need: "We are doing a third-grade unit on the rainforest, and I could use ten nonfiction books, and ten storybooks set in a rainforest." If they call ahead, you can start pulling books for teachers, who will greatly appreciate the service! This will make your job easier, too; it will help you know what topics are in demand at what grade levels, so you can purchase materials wisely. You can also show teachers books they never would have looked at, such as poetry or craft books that go with their nonfiction topics. Having teachers call ahead when they need a large number of books also allows you time to borrow books from neighboring libraries.

At other times parents need you to help find books on sensitive topics: a death in the family, sex education, divorce, or other social issues about which the parent is asking for the books, not the child. We conduct the reference interview in the usual way, with the addition of asking with what age child the parent will be using the book. Offer a wide array of books if you can, both below and above the intended grade level; the parent will know what may be best for that particular child. It can also be beneficial to have both nonfiction and fiction on the topic; a factual book on divorce may be helpful, but a story or novel in which the main character is a child whose parents are divorcing may resonant with the student who reads it. *Bibliotherapy* is the term for using a book to help someone deal with a psychological issue like a death in the family; books cannot replace discussing a problem with a caring adult but can be additional support for a parent and child during a trying time.

When a parent's request seems very out of the ordinary, such as asking for potty training books for a child who seems too young, you can point out that the books on potty training are aimed at children two and a half, not one year of age. However, it is the parents' decision to take the book. Maybe that book will help them decide the child isn't ready yet; don't insult parents by telling them they can't ask for something. Flexibility is the key when giving books to parents making a request.

REFERENCE: THE FIRST IMPRESSION

Finally, reference can be the first interaction we have with any library user. The more we come across as helpful, kind, and positive, the better chance we will have of that customer returning. Remember, you never get a second chance to make a first impression. So even if you are out of all your books on geckos, you can make the visit positive by printing out information on the Internet and showing the customer how to place a hold on gecko books. That way, he or she doesn't walk away empty handed and will visit the library again soon!

Chapter 2

Homework Help

HOMEWORK AND REFERENCE

Building on the skills covered in chapter 1, this chapter goes more in depth about helping children find homework materials in the library. Advice on communicating with schools and teachers is included. Also covered is using the Internet to assist children in finding homework information and tutoring Web sites.

Getting What They Need, Not What They Want

Often a student will come into the library and say, "I need a book about Benjamin Franklin." Follow that up by asking whether the book is needed for an assignment or to read for fun. If it is for an assignment, ask if the student has a paper from school describing the assignment. Sometimes students will ask for a book on a topic, when they really just need to write a paragraph or two on the topic or answer a few questions. In cases like that, an encyclopedia article is usually a better choice for fulfilling the assignment than a hundred-page biography. Try to offer several choices while chatting about the assignment, and it may come to light that the homework just requires a short answer, not a ten-page essay.

Finding Resources

To find materials for homework, start with your online public catalog or card catalog. Publishers are well aware of school curriculum needs and often publish series that are designed with homework and school reports in mind. For many homework topics, you will find books that will help. If you cannot find a book on an unusual topic, try encyclopedias. Offer to photocopy the pages if the book cannot be checked out of the library; many children do not have money but will need that page to do their homework. Sometimes children need some basic examples of a math problem or have other simple homework questions. For these, try the books by Anne Zeman, such as *Everything You Need to Know About Math Homework, Everything You Need to Know about Geography Homework,* and others in the series published by Scholastic Books. To find out more about this useful series, go to www.scholastic.com.

TUTORING AND HOMEWORK CENTERS

Some libraries find it possible to establish homework centers, so that latchkey children have a place to go to do their homework. A homework center doesn't necessarily have to be in the library proper; it can be in a meeting room or classroom. Often students need space to do homework but don't always need library materials aside from a dictionary and a set of encyclopedias to assist with homework, and their textbooks. So a homework center can be any additional space available, leaving the seating in the library for those students who need to use library materials.

Homework Centers Fill a Need

Many homework centers are funded by special grants, which pay for a staff member to supervise the room, pay for older high school or college students to serve as tutors, and fund computers and Internet access for the homework center. Many students do not have Internet access or a word processing computer at home, so the homework center can provide that necessity, since many middle and high school students are required to type reports. Also, many students do not have parents at home who can assist with homework because of English-language limitations or other factors. So a homework center can assist with this need as well. If a community can show there is a need, by demonstrating a certain percentage of non-English-speaking families, for example, there will be grants available to address that need. To find out more about starting a homework center at your library, check out Cindy Mediavilla's *Creating the Full-Service Homework Center in Your Library* (Chicago: American Library Association, 2001).

Information versus Instruction

A key to managing children in the library who are doing homework is to figure out whether they need information or instruction. Usually a librarian can provide information: answer a question, find a book, or spell a word. Instruction is more like tutoring, which is often outside of what the library staff can do, especially those in smaller libraries who are answering the phone, checking out materials, and running a one- or two-person operation. If a child needs tutoring, let the parents know that you are unable to provide that service and help them find alternates. Some Boys and Girls Clubs, YMCAs, and recreation departments offer after-school programs that include tutoring. If you find your community has nowhere for people to turn for homework assistance, think about establishing a homework center. Or at the least, recruit older high school students as volunteer after-school helpers who can offer simple tutoring in math or reading.

COMMUNICATING WITH SCHOOLS

If you find that there are repeated requests for homework resources that your library does not have, check with the teachers or administrators at the school. See if they can recommend books or Web sites that will fulfill that homework assignment. If they don't have any ideas, let them know you have been trying but cannot find materials for that assignment; knowing that, the teacher will likely alter the assignment or let you know what books the library should purchase. See if the teachers or office staff at the school can fax or e-mail assignment information to you in advance so you can purchase more materials or borrow from other libraries, especially for assignments expected of the entire seventh grade, for example. You can also set aside books on a certain topic for in-library use only, if you have advance notice that a large number of students will be needing these books at the same time.

HOMESCHOOLERS

Homeschoolers can be devoted library users if you welcome them and let the parents know you will offer them the same services you offer any other teacher. Encourage them to come for a library tour; see if they can coordinate with some other homeschoolers to come for a tour together so you have more than a couple of students to speak to during the tour. Encourage them to request materials in advance of assignments; you may need to borrow some items from a larger library or system if the homeschooling curriculum differs from the local public schools, which often happens. Let them know if there are times that are not good for visits, as well as times that are good; many homeschoolers understand you cannot give them much help on Tuesday mornings because you have preschool storytime, so they will come on another morning if you let them know the library's schedule.

USE OF THE WEB

The Internet may be useful for some student research questions but not all. Sometimes it is more useful to find books on ducks for second graders doing an animal report, because nearly everything on the Web will be too difficult for them to read. And searching "ducks" will lead you to hockey teams as well as the animal. If a child needs to look up the capital of a country, the almanac may be faster. When doing the reference interview, ask whether the teacher specified that this homework assignment be done using books only, or if the teacher wants the student to use the Internet. Sometimes the teacher will have specified a particular Web site to visit.

A great resource on using the Internet with kids is *Delivering Web Reference Services to Young People,* by Walter Minkel and Roxanne Hsu Feldman (Chicago: American Library Association, 1999). Not only does this helpful, concise guide show you how to use the Web for homework help, it also explains how to teach Web research skills to young people and how to set up a library Web site.

The Internet can be a great resource for small libraries that don't have enough books for every sixth grader who walks over from the local school, especially when all 150 of them are doing the same project. The Internet won't have everything, however, due to copyright laws. Students who all need the same poem may not find it on the Internet. Or students who all need the same article from *Time* magazine may find that paper copy issue checked out, and the article only available online from a paid database resource such as Infotrac. For more general homework research assignments, the Internet will have photographs and information to supplement book resources.

Because too much of what is on the Internet cannot be verified as fact, using a search engine or subject directory that is proven to be helpful to students can ensure the child is walking away with accurate information. The ones used most often with elementary school students are:

> Yahooligans (http://www.yahooligans.com). The children's version of Yahoo, a handy search engine to help them find homework answers, pictures to print, etc. Especially good for popular culture (music, TV shows, cartoons, movies).

> KidsClick (http://www.kidsclick.org). A wealth of links to homework-helpful sites, all selected by children's librarians. The Web page is arranged in categories just like the Dewey Decimal system.

> Ask Jeeves for Kids (http://www.ajkids.com). Students can ask specific questions, such as, "What is the fastest animal in North America?" as well as find links to almanacs, atlases, and dictionaries. Children can also click on the subject they need assistance with, for instance, math, and find help.

> Google (http://www.google.com). Even though this isn't designed for children, many students use Google to find pictures they can print to use for reports. Librarians may need to give

more guidance to students using Google, since the user has to sift through sites that don't have what is needed.

Many people, adults and children alike, tend to believe everything they read on the Internet. With some search tools, for example KidsClick!, you can be fairly confident that what they find is true, because librarians have chosen all the links on that site. But if a student uses a different search engine, you may want to do more follow-up to see that the student found what was needed. You can see whether the site was created by an educational group such as National Geographic (which is the largest nonprofit scientific and educational institution in the world) or by a commercial entity just trying to sell something. You can do this by casually asking if the student found what was needed, or if the student would like you to check to make sure the correct information was found.

USE OF COMPUTERS

Students don't need library computers just for the Internet. Many young people do not have a computer at home for them to do word processing or work in other programs. More schools are requiring that homework be done in Word or other programs that can create a typed report. Access to free computers at the library may be a student's only resource. Encourage your library to have some computers just for children and teens to use after school or on weekends, so that they can complete a typed homework assignment. Also, check with students periodically to see if they are using the computer in an efficient manner. For example, on a home computer the student can type a paragraph, read a source, and type some more. But on a library computer, the clock is ticking, so a student should be prepared with a handwritten rough draft, ready to type. Students as young as fourth grade may be required to type reports, so access to a computer will be essential to their success, and the local library may be the only place they can get that.

HOMEWORK ON THE INCREASE

Parents will tell you that even their younger children have more homework than they did just a few years ago; this is especially true of middle and high school students. And since many students do not see their parents until dinnertime when the parents get home from work, students spend a lot of time in the afternoon doing homework without the help of a parent. In many communities, the library has become the place where children go to start on homework until parents get home from work, so library staff and volunteers are needed for more homework assistance than in the past. This can even involve explaining how to do a math problem, or other homework that does not require library resources. Because testing related to the No Child Left Behind legislation takes up more classroom time than in the past, children spend more time on homework that used to be done in the classroom. The library staff needs to become more proficient at providing help for homework. That could mean the librarian needs to communicate with the school so we can be better at offering homework assistance. Some librarians work out a partnership, in which the local school has noncirculating copies of textbooks at the library for students to refer to in case they left their copy of the textbook at school. Many librarians use e-mail to communicate with teachers and to receive homework alert notices so the library can set aside a "reserve shelf" for specific assignments required of a large number of students. Librarians are trying to be more proactive in preparing for homework by communicating with teachers, by recruiting older teen and adult volunteers, and by offering Internet and computers for word processing for students who do not have these resources at home. Helping with homework is becoming a bigger part of the librarian's job, so being prepared will just make our jobs easier.

Chapter 3

Readers' Advisory

OFFERING READING SUGGESTIONS

Many librarians and paraprofessionals who work at the Children's Desk have a love of reading and an appreciation for children's books that led them to this career. Even if you do not know children's books well right now, this chapter will help you learn skills to assist children in finding recreational reading, including tips on the readers' advisory interview, an overview of children's fiction and reading levels, how to "market" children's books with booktalks and booklists, and reference books and Web sites useful in helping children find recreational reading. This chapter covers special topics in recreational reading, including paperback series books, multicultural fiction, and encouraging both boys and girls to find books they enjoy.

Library staff and volunteers at all levels, from your library aides who shelve books to the library director, probably came to work in a library because they loved reading. They enjoy fiction and novels and often were the kind of child who would read under the covers with a flashlight. So doing readers' advisory can tap into their passion for books. You don't need to have read every book in the children's room to do readers' advisory, but it does take some interpersonal communication skills, like being a good listener and being patient. Connecting children with books that soon become their favorites can be very rewarding.

Readers' advisory is usually thought of as finding recreational reading, as opposed to finding books for homework assignments or books on how to draw or play a sport. So readers' advisory often means finding fiction books for the customer, similar to hand-selling in an independent bookstore. It can be very challenging, like picking out clothes for someone you don't know. This can be made even more difficult if the child is not there. Sometimes parents are in the library to pick up books to read for fun for their children; but the children aren't there to add their input. While this is more difficult, it can be done. In fact, children are often more flexible in their recreational reading than adults. We all have an aunt or grandmother who only reads mysteries, but a child who may be a huge fantasy or Harry Potter fan will try a novel set in history like Scott O'Dell's *Island of the Blue Dolphins* or an animal story like Sheila Burnford's *The Incredible Journey*. Children often will branch out in their reading choices.

READERS' ADVISORY INTERVIEW

When first being asked for reading recommendations, you should find out whether what is wanted is a book to read "for fun" or for homework. If it is for homework, the teacher may have said the book had to be at least a certain length, perhaps 100 pages. The teacher also may have specified that it be from a list, or that it be a Newbery-winning novel. A teacher may also specify that it be a mystery, or historical fiction, or a "classic," so determining if the request is for a book report for school will lead you to regular reference interview questions such as, "Do you have the handout from your teacher describing the assignment?" Sometimes, even when reading for "fun" children need a book from a reading incentive program like Accelerated Reader or Scholastic Reading Counts! (SRC), and not all books are on these lists.

If it is determined that the request is for a book for fun and not specifically related to homework, there are several questions you can ask to help discover the patron's reading interests. Begin by asking if he or she can recall a recent book read for fun. If the answer is *Ramona* by Beverly

Cleary, you can offer other books by that author. Or, you can offer other humorous contemporary novels with a quirky girl main character, such as Barbara Park's Junie B. Jones, Megan McDonald's Judy Moody, or Paula Danziger's Amber Brown. Whatever book is named will help you know the child's reading level. Next, ask what grade the child is in. That may tell you what the child can handle in the way of social issues and can help give an indication of reading level, but not always, since some children in the same grade read way below or way above grade level. Also ask if the book is for that person, because some children visit the library to obtain books for a sibling. If it is the parent, you may want to ask if it is for a boy or girl, because sometimes gender plays a part in what type of books are requested, especially for children ages eight and above.

TYPES OF BOOKS

Just like a salesperson at a store, the library staff person should know a little something about the different categories in which children's books are shelved. That way, when offering readers' advisory, and the person wants a book about dogs, you can follow up by finding out what type of dog book: a nonfiction book on training a new puppy, a picture book for a very young child, an easy reader such as Norman Bridwell's Clifford series, a novel like *Shiloh* by Phyllis Reynolds Naylor, or a book of poetry about dogs. The categories for children's books found in most libraries include picture books, board books, picture books for older readers, easy readers, transitional fiction, fiction, nonfiction, and graphic novels. Each of these is discussed briefly below.

Picture Books

Picture books are usually thirty-two pages long, oversized books with illustrations on every page, for example, Maurice Sendak's *Where the Wild Things Are* or Ludwig Bemelmans's *Madeline*. In most cases, these are made for the parent to read to the child, not the child to read on his or her own. These are used by a wide age range, including babies, toddlers, preschoolers, kindergartners, and even primary graders.

Board Books

Libraries did not always carry board books; they were thought of as books for those under eighteen months, to be read by a parent and chewed on or dropped in the bathtub by a baby. But many libraries now carry board books and even use them in their baby storytimes; board books have cardboard covers and pages. They are not always easy to read but are very short, often with twelve pages or fewer, and very clear, uncluttered illustrations. Stay away from the board books that are adapted from picture books, because too often they are abridged. When they are not abridged, they are often too wordy for this audience.

Picture Books for Older Readers

This is a new category in many libraries, due to the publication of sophisticated picture books that are not appropriate for preschoolers. These picture books are usually thirty-two pages long and fully illustrated like regular preschool picture books, but the content demands an older child to understand the story. An example of this is Walter Dean Myers's *Patrol: An American Soldier in Vietnam*, a picture book about the Vietnam War. It may frighten a young child, but a third grader can appreciate the story. Another example is Patricia Polacco's *Pink and Say*, set during the U.S. Civil War.

Easy Readers

When children are learning how to read, there are great books to help them, with exciting illustrations that will assist in guessing the vocabulary. Think of Dr. Seuss's *Green Eggs and Ham* or Arnold Lobel's *Frog and Toad*. Smaller than picture books, with more white space on the page, easy readers can be fun and exciting.

Transitional Fiction

One of the more difficult types of books to find is a book that is more challenging than *Green Eggs and Ham* but not as demanding as a chapter book such as E. B. White's *Charlotte's Web*. These "moving up" books can be as easy as James Howe's *Pinky and Rex* or as fun as Dav Pilkey's *The Adventures of Captain Underpants*. You have to try the books on; have the child look at a page: too much writing or just right?

Not enough white space; is the text too small? The *Magic Treehouse* series by Mary Pope Osborne is very popular with this grade level.

Fiction

Once transitional chapter books are too easy, most children leap into the world of fiction that spans E. B. White's *Charlotte's Web* to J. K. Rowlings's *Harry Potter* series. Most Newbery Award books are fiction, which adults would call novels. When children reach fourth and fifth grade, most can read these with ease and want to choose for themselves. By this age, they start to have very specific tastes in recreational reading, and will seek out fantasy, mysteries, or other genres.

Nonfiction

Not just for homework anymore: many children read nonfiction for fun. Whether on cars, dinosaurs, or baseball players, nonfiction books with photos and other visuals appeal to many children, especially to boys who may not be ready for longer novels.

Graphic Novels

In some ways, graphic novels look like comic books, with dialogue balloons and panel full-color artwork. However, these are much longer than comic books, with a lengthy plot and more characters. Older children and teens are especially interested in graphic novels, whether they have superheroes or are Manga, which are based on Japanese animation. Even though they look like comics, some graphic novels are only appropriate for high school students and adults due to sexual content and violence, so check out the recommended grade level at www.bwibooks. com before offering them to younger children.

GRADE/READING LEVELS

When offering readers' advisory, it can be difficult to figure out a child's reading level. Just asking what grade a student is in can help a little but is not enough. Ask if the child can name others books he or she has read recently; the child may be as tall as you are but could still be reading transitional fiction instead of longer novels.

Paperback Books

If you are helping children in the paperback racks, look at the back cover of the book. Most children's paperbacks have an RL (for reading level) followed by a number. That will give you an idea at what grade level it is aimed: RL 3.5 means the book is for the average child halfway through third grade.

The Five-Finger Rule

One of the most difficult reading levels to determine is for the child learning how to read. The easy readers will often have a number one, two, or three on the cover to help. You discern that it is for the beginning, middle, or near the end of first grade. You can also use the "five-finger" rule for easy readers. Take the child aside (and away from others so there is no chance to embarrass anyone) and have the child read the first page to you. If a child needs help with a few words, that is fine, it means the book is somewhat challenging. If help is needed with more than five words (hold up a finger every time you have to tell the child a word), then the book is too difficult and will turn the child away from reading.

One Size Does Not Fit All

Not all fourth graders will read the same books. Some will read Harry Potter and some still like shorter, easy chapter books. See what "fits" each child. Also, some children can read way above their levels, perhaps the fourth grader who reads Harry Potter. Instead of offering that person Tolkien's *The Hobbit,* as you would a seventh-grade Potter fan, offer longer novels that are more on a fourth grader's interest level, such as Brian Jacques's Redwall series or Edward Eager's *Half Magic.*

Nonfiction Levels May Be Higher

Many children who ask for nonfiction books will appreciate books above their grade level, because they want to look at the photographs. Also, if the subject, such as dinosaurs, is of special interest to children, the books will be read even though much of the vocabulary is a level or more above what they normally read. Offer a wide variety of reading levels when showing nonfiction books; children will pick out things that interest them and will find things they can read.

GENRES OF FICTION

Similar to fiction for adults, chapter books for children often fall into specific categories. Unlike adults, children will read across genres quite readily. Some of the first children's books were fantasy: L. Frank Baum's *The Wizard of Oz,* Lewis Carroll's *Alice in Wonderland,* among others. Historical fiction was also popular early on, with Howard Pyle's books based on Arthurian legends. But many genres—fantasy, science fiction, contemporary realistic fiction, humor, mystery/horror/gothic, sports, animals, adventure, historical fiction, and multicultural fiction—are available in children's fiction, so let's just touch on the popular authors and distinctive qualities of these genres.

Fantasy

Fantasy seems often to be inspired by traditional folktales, such as Hans Christian Andersen's original tales, including *The Little Mermaid* and *The Ugly Duckling,* which have strong fairy tale motifs but are really modern fantasy. J. R. R. Tolkien's books; C. S. Lewis's Narnia series; and the wonderful books by Lloyd Alexander, Ursula LeGuin, and Susan Cooper, all have folktale elements of witches, little people, and dragons. Then there are books with characters who have magical powers, such as J. K. Rowling's Harry Potter books, Mary Norton's The Borrowers, Lucy Boston's Green Knowe books, and many others. These use traditional magical beings and add them to original plots.

Another popular setting for fantasy is animals that talk. Kenneth Grahame's *Wind in the Willows* isn't as popular as it once was, but it is a great example of this genre, as are A. A. Milne's Winnie the Pooh books, E. B. White's books, George Selden's *The Cricket in Times Square,* and Avi's Poppy series.

Humorous fantasy takes the real world and adds magic to make fun of the stuffy, overly serious world of adults. Astrid Lindgren's *Pippi Longstocking* and P. L. Travers' *Mary Poppins* are examples of humorous fantasy. The early Harry Potter books also fall into this category.

Science Fiction

A subgenre of fantasy, science fiction (sci fi) was not readily found in children's books until relatively recently. Children read books by Jules Verne, but he didn't write specifically for them. Children also read science fiction comic books. But Madeleine L'Engle's *A Wrinkle in Time* really opened the door. Her work is still popular, and inspired William Sleator, John Christopher, and others. Many adult sci fi authors also wrote books just for children, including Andre Norton, Isaac Asimov, Robert Heinlein, and others.

Contemporary Realistic Fiction

One of the largest and most popular genres, contemporary realistic fiction for children includes family stories, school stories, problem stories, and just about anything else that doesn't fall into one of the other genres. This genre includes more multicultural characters and themes, and can address topical issues like AIDS, terrorism, and poverty. These books can also open children's minds to gender issues, nontraditional families, and other political themes. The best realistic fiction has strong characters, important themes, truthful depictions, and a believable first person voice (if that is being used), and doesn't pander to children or underestimate their intelligence. These books can meet a child's need to know, need to belong, need for security, and other sensitive topics. Mark Twain and Louisa May Alcott, thought of as historical fiction authors now, were the forerunners of modern, realistic fiction for young people.

Eleanor Estes's books were often set in the city, almost a children's version of stories like Betty Smith's *A Tree Grows in Brooklyn.* Estes's *Hundred Dresses* is a poignant look at prejudice. Beverly Cleary's humorous chapter books also addressed issues in a subtle way; for example, in *Ramona and Her Father,* Dad is unemployed. Louise Fitzhugh's *Harriet the Spy* deals with gender identity, Judy Blume's books often address issues such as puberty, and E. L. Konigsburg's and S. E. Hinton's books often discuss "fitting in." Many of these books address realistic, controversial issues, but temper them with humor and thoughtfulness. Even books about death such as Lois Lowry's *A Summer to Die* offer hope.

Humor

An offshoot of realistic fiction is humorous fiction, although there are also humorous fantasy novels, mysteries, and so forth. Great humor is difficult to achieve, but when it is done well, it can be very popular with all children, especially as a classroom or family read-aloud. Examples of realistic humor include Betsy Byars's <u>Bingo Brown</u> books, Lois Lowry's books about Anastasia Krupnik and her brother Sam, and Barbara Robinson's books about the horrible Herdman's. Fantasy humor includes Mary Rodger's *Freaky Friday.* Historical fiction that is humorous includes many books by Sid Fleischman, including the gold rush-era adventure *By The Great Horn Spoon!* (three genres in one—humor, adventure, and historical fiction!).

Mystery/Horror/Gothic

When asked which books they read as children, many children's authors and librarians will answer <u>Nancy Drew and the Hardy Boys.</u> These mystery series were thought to be "chewing gum for the mind," but were popular when they first came out and are still popular now. In fact, mystery series in general are still popular, from <u>Cam Jansen</u> to <u>Encyclopedia Brown</u> to <u>Sammy Keyes.</u> Newbery Medalist Laurence Yep has created a series set in San Francisco's Chinatown, featuring a Chinese American girl detective, sort of a Chinese American Nancy Drew, and Betsy Byars created Herculeah Jones. Children's mystery stories are often set in the here and now, but some are also historical fiction, including Philip Pullman's *Ruby in the Smoke,* set in Victorian England.

Mysteries can appeal to children who don't like "reading," because of the suspense. The best mysteries will have probable plots, clues to help the reader solve the mystery, foreshadowing that is not too obvious, and great pacing and suspense. Many children also like the "scary" element of some mysteries. One of the most popular series currently in bookstores and libraries are the books about the Baudelaire orphans, by "Lemony Snicket," also known as San Franciscan Dan Handler.

Sports

Too often, sports novels offer formulaic plots with too much on-field or on-court action, so character development suffers. But the best sports novels for youth, such as Bruce Brooks's *The Moves Make the Man,* offer both believable characters, exciting action, and realistic plots. The best-known sports author is probably the late Matt Christopher; his books are formulaic but popular. John Tunis was an early proponent of the sports novel for youth, and Scott Corbett and Alfred Slote also wrote for this genre. R. R. Knudson is one of the few women writers of the sports novel, and her books offer female protagonists and very realistic sports action.

Animals

Talking animal stories such as E. B. White's *Charlotte's Web* are fantasy. The realistic animal story is equally popular. Examples include *Old Yeller* by Fred Gipson, Phyllis Reynolds Naylor's <u>Shiloh</u> series, and books by Jean Craighead George or Walt Morey. In these books, the animals are realistically portrayed, but they offer readers a chance to involve their emotions. Most of the animal novels seem to focus on dogs or horses, and cats or other animals to a lesser degree. The best of these don't manipulate one's emotions, but offer universal truths and realistic characters.

Adventure

Many adventure stories are also historical fiction, from Robert Louis Stevenson's *Treasure Island* to the books by Leon Garfield and Iain Lawrence. They are action-packed stories, often set at sea, featuring pirates, explorers, journeys and quests, and villains. Some adventure books are set in the present, and feature a boy or girl who has to survive in the wilderness; Gary Paulsen's *Hatchet* is a great example. The adventure story can have heightened realism and less ambiguous heroes and villains than realistic fiction, but both historical and modern adventures should at least be possible, if not probable, to be believable.

Historical Fiction

Historical fiction is one of the oldest and most popular genres in children's fiction. From the autobiographical novels of Laura Ingalls Wilder, to the many books by Scott O'Dell, and the recent work by Karen Cushman, this genre offers books that even adults can read and admire. In fact, adult reading circles are using Karen Hesse's *Out of the Dust*. Some books we think of as historical fiction were actually realistic fiction at the time they were written; Louisa May Alcott's *Little Women* comes to mind. Historical fiction is very dramatic, with great characters, but must be historically accurate to be truly notable. Children may not be able to catch the errors, but the accurate historical novel can add to a child's understanding of history, and shouldn't require the reader to bring too much knowledge of the time period to be able to understand the story.

Historical fiction offers exciting, dramatic plots, and often a clear sense of right and wrong. But authors need to have the characters speak in a realistic way for that time period, and not sound like contemporary children. Cornelia Meigs and Rachel Fields were two children's book authors in the early 1900s who wrote historical fiction. They were followed by Marguerite de Angeli (*Door in the Wall*) and Elizabeth Coatsworth. Others who are still read include Elizabeth George Speare (*Witch of Blackbird Pond*), Rosemary Sutcliff, and Esther Forbes (*Johnny Tremain*).

The Scott O'Dell Award, named after the author of *Island of the Blue Dolphins,* is given to a book for children that is historical fiction. A look at the list of Newbery Medal and Honor books shows that many are historical fiction for grades five to eight; it seems to be a very popular genre. Of course, school librarians and teachers see the added factor that historical fiction can bring to the classroom: it can offer great literature and a love of reading while conveying information that also relates to the history and social studies curriculum. It seems as though most historical fiction for children is set in Europe or in the United States, but there is also historical fiction that represents the non-Western world. In 2002, the Newbery Medal went to *A Single Shard* by Linda Sue Park, which is set in medieval Korea.

FICTION SERIES

For children old enough to read chapter books, fiction series are often their first recreational reading choice. Some series are very well written, such as Redwall by Brian Jacques, and others are more formulaic, like R. L. Stine's Goosebumps. But these books are aimed at children age eight and above, when they should be allowed some choices in recreational reading. Sure, some are the literary equivalent of dessert, but, while you don't want children to eat ice cream as their only food, once in a while is fine. *Popular Series Fiction for K–6 Readers: A Reading and Selection Guide* by Rebecca L. Thomas and Catherine Barr (Westport,

CT: Libraries Unlimited, 2005) is a helpful guide that lists series books. More than 1,000 series are listed in the guide, along with annotations and lists of the titles in the series in number order.

Another helpful resource is a Web site that lists popular children's series fiction—www.mcpl.lib.mo.us/readers/series/juv/—provided by the Mid-Continent Public Library in Missouri. This handy Web site can be searched by series name, individual book title, author, and subject.

MULTICULTURAL FICTION

Children of color do not see themselves portrayed in movies, television, or books as often as they see white children. It is important that they see themselves in books; in fact, even Anglo American children should see all types of cultures represented in their books to see the diversity of our country. When doing readers' advisory, offer a wide variety of books representing different cultures to all children. Don't just offer books by African American authors to black children; if you only offer books by Christopher Paul Curtis or Elizabeth Fitzgerald Howard to black children, everyone else misses out on great books. Be sure your library has a wide selection of books that represent the many ethnic groups you serve, and even have books on cultures that may not yet live in your community.

When children see themselves in books, hopefully they see positive images of their gender, their cultures, and their ethnicities. But this was not always so. Until the 1960s, it was unusual to see a nonwhite child in a children's book, unless the depiction was for historical reasons (for example, Jim in Mark Twain's *The Adventures of Huckleberry Finn*), or the nonwhites were portrayed in a stereotypical manner, such as the illustrations in *Little Black Sambo*. But Janice Udry's picture books about Mary Jo were readily found on library shelves during President Kennedy's administration. The books of Don Freeman (*Corduroy*), Leo Politi, and Ezra Jack Keats featured nonwhite children even though the authors were of European descent. Sometimes these multicultural books had themes of brotherhood or specific ethnic issues, but sometimes they were about everyday subjects. In Ezra Jack Keats's *The Snowy Day,* the characters just happened to be African American. The acceptance of multicultural characters by the picture book genre wasn't as readily apparent in fiction for older children; there were a few nonwhite chapter book characters but not many, and usually written by nonwhite authors. It wasn't until the 1970s, with the work of Virginia Hamilton and Mildred Taylor, that we saw African American children's fiction. One of the most notable African American authors for young people is Walter Dean Myers; many of his books are classified as Young Adult, but children ages ten to twelve also read his work. Now his son, Christopher Myers, has entered the publishing world as a talented author and illustrator of picture books.

The contribution of Asian American authors seems to be reserved to a smaller pool: Laurence Yep, Allen Say, Yoshiko Uchida, Lensey Namioka, An Na, Linda Sue Park, Janet Wong, Cynthia Kadohata, and just a few others. Hopefully, more will break through the publishing "glass ceiling." Also, publishing house Lee and Low focuses on multicultural picture books, including Asian American authors and illustrators, so hopefully we will see more new creations.

Although there is not a large number of Native American Indian authors, a few are receiving great reviews, and their books are increasingly used in classrooms and public libraries. Joseph Bruchac has published novels and folklore; he is from the Abenaki tribe and is also a renowned storyteller. Louise Erdrich, known for her adult novels and poetry, has written two children's books, *The Birchback House* and *The Game of Silence,* featuring a young Ojibwe girl named Omakayas, set in 1850. Cynthia Leitich Smith's books, including *Jingle Dancer,* are unique because they are about contemporary Native American children. She is a member of the Muskogee (Creek) nation.

The contribution of Hispanic/Latino authors and illustrators seems to be divided into East and West coast; the East coast (where nearly all publishers are based) features many more Cuban and Puerto Rican authors, and the West Coast features more Mexican American authors. For a long time, only the East Coast talent was getting published. Thankfully, Mexican American children now can read great books by Gary Soto, David Diaz, Francisco Jimenez, and a few others. One West Coast phenomenon has added greatly to the availability of children's books for the Spanish-speaking community: Children's Book Press. Started more than twenty-five years ago by Harriet Rohmer in the San Francisco Bay Area, Children's Book Press is a nonprofit publisher (www.childrensbookpress.org). Its books are usually picture books, but they appeal to a wide age range and are often printed with both English and another language on the page. The bulk have been from Latin American cultures, both folktales and original stories. The press has branched out to include African American and Asian cultures as well. Its focus on Pacific Rim bilingual books has filled a gap that no one else has bothered to address, and the press has the awards to show that this has been a worthy cause.

Other small presses also offer the works of multicultural authors. Cinco Puntos Press (http://www.cincopuntos.com/) specializes in bilingual books celebrating Latino culture. Oyate, a Native American nonprofit organization (http://www.oyate.org), reviews books on Native American culture and has several lists of recommended books for children.

Black Books Galore! Guide to Great African American Children's Books by Donna Rand, Toni Trent Parker, and Sheila Foster (New York: John Wiley & Sons, 1998) is a lively listing of books for children written by African Americans and featuring positive, nonstereotypical African American characters.

Latina and Latino Voices in Literature for Children and Teenagers by Frances Ann Day (Portsmouth, NH: Heinemann, 1997) is arranged by the children's book authors' and illustrators' names. This complete look at the current state of Latino authors for youth talks about the books as well as having biographical information about the creators.

Awards for multicultural children's books include the Coretta Scott King Award for African American children's authors and illustrators and the Pura Belpre Award for Hispanic/Latino children's authors and illustrators. To find the lists of these award winners, visit the American Library Association's Web site at www.ala.org.

GENDER ISSUES

When kids get to be old enough to read novels on their own, they often will want books with a boy main character if the reader is a boy and a girl protagonist if the reader is a girl. Not all children react this way; it can depend on the book. The average boy will not want a book with a pink cover that has the word "princess" on it, but many boys like the Ramona books by Beverly Cleary. Offer all types of books so children will figure out what works for them. If you are not helping the child but rather a parent who is seeking books for a fourth or fifth grader, you can ask if it is a boy or girl since that may help you offer more specific choices.

BIBLIOTHERAPY

At times parents may want a book for their children to help with the death of a grandparent, an impending divorce, or another issue. This is referred to as bibliotherapy. A book won't be the only counseling a child may need if his or her parents are divorcing, but books can help in the process or motivate a child to discuss the problem with a parent. Usually the online catalog can help you find books on these issues by searching under the subject and then looking for fiction on that subject.

RELUCTANT READERS

Reluctant readers is a term, often used by teachers, for children who read below grade level or children who just don't like reading even if they do read on grade level. Reluctant readers can be like picky eaters; they are more "choosy" about what they will read, so we have to help them find something they like. Many reluctant readers will be more open to looking at magazines and comics, because the visual design is more inviting than a page of solid text. Some like nonfiction and will read an informational book on a subject they are interested in, for example dinosaurs, cars and planes, or animals, if the book has great color photos. Find out what interests them and offer something on that topic: if they are video gamers, offer electronic gaming magazines. Some reluctant readers would rather read text on a computer screen than on a paper page, so we know they can read. The readers' advisory interview with a reluctant reader will take more time, but once you find out a child's hobby or interest, you can usually get him or her to take a book or magazine on that topic.

HELPFUL TOOLS FOR READERS' ADVISORY

Until you have time to build your own knowledge of books and before you have read many children's books yourself, it can be difficult to think of books even if you know the child you are helping likes mysteries, or fantasy, or realistic fiction. But there are books and Web sites that will help you find books on those interests.

Book Adventure (www.bookadventure.org) offers a great search tool to find books on almost any topic, and you can limit the search by grade level. Go to the Kids' Zone, then select Book Finder. There, you can choose fiction or nonfiction, pick a grade level, and pick up to five different topics you would like books on, including genres like adventure or humor, topics like animals or sports, or themes like friendship. The Web site also has quizzes teachers can use to reward reading comprehension. The Web site is sponsored by Sylvan Learning.

Award-winning author Jon Scieszka, who used to be a second-grade teacher, has a Web site that lists great books to recommend to boys (www.guysread.com). Many educators see a gender divide in reading: boys read less than girls and often read below grade level to a greater degree than girls. The Guys Read Web site has lists of great books to recommend to boys, as well as advice for librarians, teachers, and parents on getting boys interested in books.

Another great resource is *Best Books for Children: Preschool through Grade 6,* 8th ed., by Catherine Barr and John T. Gillespie (Westport, CT: Libraries Unlimited, 2005). Organized thematically, more than 25,000 books are described and recommended for children.

Also try *Valerie and Walter's Best Books for Children: A Lively, Opinionated Guide, Revised and Updated* by Valerie V. Lewis and Walter M. Mayes (New York: HarperCollins, 2004). Two book experts offer thousands of reading recommendations for kids and teens, arranged by age level. The subject index is very detailed, and the annotations are often very funny and insightful.

One of the experts in this field is children's librarian Kathleen Odean. She has published several guides to finding good books for children. Try *Great Books for Boys,* (New York: Ballantine, 1998). She lists over 600 books recommended for boys, arranged by genre such as adventure, sports, and fantasy, and her booklist is annotated. She also has a new edition of *Great Books for Girls* (New York: Ballantine, 2002). Revised from her 1991 edition, it offers hundreds of recreational reading suggestions aimed at girls.

BOOKTALKS

When classes or groups come for a library tour, you can "booktalk" books you are suggesting for check out. Booktalking can be very effective with classes of older elementary and middle school students, as a way to advertise great new novels. Think of a booktalk as a "sneak preview" or a commercial for the book; you don't want to give away the ending, but tell just enough about the plot to give listeners an idea of what the book is about. A booktalk is usually a minute or two in length, giving a brief description of the major characters and the basic plot (but never the ending!), as well as the tone of the book. Read out loud a paragraph of the book, especially one that ends in a cliff-hanger, the way a movie preview gets viewers interested in buying a ticket to that movie by leading viewers up to, but not over, the edge of the action. Many books offer written booktalks, including Joni Bodart's *Booktalk! Five* (H.W. Wilson, 1993). Also try *Booktalking That Works* by Jennifer Bromann (New York: Neal-Schuman, 2001). Although this is aimed at Young Adult librarians, children's library staff members can use the information to write and tell great booktalks to get children to read for fun.

BOOKLISTS

Even in this age of the Internet, many librarians still find it useful to have paper lists of best sellers, or recommended books, that parents, teachers, and children can refer to for ideas on what to read next. Sometimes the booklists are seasonal: picture books for children starting school, scary books for Halloween, December holiday books, or summer reading suggestions. Many librarians offer lists of great new books recommended by grade level: new easy readers for first and second graders, new short chapter books for third and fourth graders, new novels for fifth and sixth graders, or new nonfiction books for middle school. You can also make booklists of "read-alikes," for example, books to recommend to fans of Harry Potter who are looking for books that are similar. Suggestions that follow will help you make up these paper booklists so they will work as appealing readers' advisory tools.

Journalism is really the type of writing we do for bibliographies. We want to give the who, what, when, where, and how, in the fewest words. And we want to write as if we are writing advertising copy; we are "selling" the books by describing the stories with active verbs, creating the "I need that" impulse in our customers. Active verbs: "He struggled, overcoming the challenge of being alone in the forest with only a hatchet to help him make shelter, find food, and defend himself from wild animals" would be enough to sell Gary Paulsen's adventure novel, *Hatchet.* Make it short and snappy, but don't give away the ending (or which character dies!). But don't mislead the reader: if it is a sad book, help to indicate that so kids aren't expecting a laugh fest. If you include a sentence describing the book, that is an annotated booklist.

Don't forget, you can also make a useful booklist that doesn't have annotations, so long as the "headlines" are clear about what books are listed. Make a list of "Great Books for Guys" and a list of "Great Books for Girls," broken down by grade level, but without descriptions of the books. These look more like a shopping list. Users may ask you to describe the book or may find the title or cover appealing and not need to hear what the book is about.

In summary, writing annotations is like writing menu descriptions or advertising copy; they should be short, snappy, catchy, and active. An annotation must not give away the ending under any circumstances, yet it must play fair to let the child know if the book is a tear-jerker or not appropriate for certain grade levels due to violence, sex, or other issues. One way of writing an annotation is to use a method used in Hollywood to describe movies and TV shows: try to break it down to the "high concept." That means using clear buzz words that evoke an image: *Miami Vice* was called "MTV cops"; Goosebumps are funny, scary stories with unexpected endings like *The Twilight Zone. Out of the Dust* by Karen Hesse is a poignant story of a girl and her father surviving the Dust Bowl and poverty of the Great Depression. I am sure you can think of other examples. I often like to write the annotation in the form of a question: for example, for Natalie Babbitt's *Tuck Everlasting*: "Will Winnie drink from the fountain of youth so she can stay young forever and be with Jesse Tuck, and will they outwit the evil man in the yellow suit who is following them?" One thing I find helpful to remember is that annotation writing isn't a literary endeavor, it is journalism.

READERS' ADVISORY EQUALS JOB SATISFACTION

Many of us went into the library profession because we loved books and reading. When we match up a young reader with a book he or she comes to love, it can give us great job satisfaction. What can be better than to lead a child to a title that becomes his or her favorite book? Readers' advisory gets easier the longer you are on the job; to be really proficient, you should expect to read lots of great children's books so you can offer advice on great books and reading. But after all, reading was a hobby that probably led you to working in a library!

Chapter 4

Book Selection

A LIBRARY'S COLLECTION

Even if a library has great programs and a friendly staff, few patrons will want to borrow books if the library doesn't have what they want and need. A library's collection is carefully selected rather than acquired in a haphazard approach; the purchasing and maintaining of items is an essential service. That can be even more important in the children's room, since it is the main source for both homework and recreational reading because children have less money to spend on books than adults. Smaller libraries may have limited purchasing budgets, but they need to buy more than just the latest Newbery and Caldecott winners. This chapter provides practical advice on using book reviewing journals for collection development, vendors and Web sites for purchasing media for the children's room, tips on weeding to keep the collection relevant, and special advice on finding materials to reflect our multicultural communities and meet the needs of our students who may be learning English as a second language.

COLLECTION POLICY

First, check to see if the library has a formal, written collection policy. It may spell out certain standards that will influence what books and media are purchased. Some collection policies spell out that the library does not carry abridged works or adaptations; others may dictate that teacher requests are a top priority. While the policy for a school library says that curriculum needs come first and recreational reading second, that is not necessarily true at a public library. A public library may carry more media for patrons to check out; a school library may or may not. Some libraries rely on interlibrary loan for requests; others may prefer to purchase materials that are requested if the books are in print. Some libraries that do not have a written policy may have an informal one. Try to find out what the informal policy is should there be one.

EVALUATE THE COLLECTION

Another first step, before you begin purchasing materials, is to evaluate the collection. I like to begin by shelf reading the collection. This means you are rearranging the shelves so that books are in their correct order: fiction by author's last name and nonfiction by Dewey Decimal Classification number. When you are checking the order of books on the shelves, you will see what areas are gathering dust from lack of use and what areas are out of order, which is likely due to heavy usage. While shelf reading, you can also see if some areas have too many out-of-date books; this can happen in the science and technology nonfiction area since those books become dated more quickly than books on other topics. As you go through, you may see that the previous librarian may have purchased more new material on some topics but not on others, so now you can compensate for that to "even out" the collection. Both nonfiction and fiction need evaluation; maybe the fiction section is too dependent on old classics and award winners and needs more new, popular material such as graphic novels.

When evaluating the collection, check into circulation figures. You may find that some topics are not checked out as often as they should be; if your picture books aren't circulating, starting a weekly preschool storytime should help that. If the children's fiction for grades three to six is not checked out, a reading incentive program, perhaps a Summer

Reading Program, will greatly increase circulation in that area. Or it may be that there are not enough new books in those sections. In nonfiction, there may be many great poetry books gathering dust. Perhaps the local schools' curriculum no longer covers poetry, so doing a special display in April for National Poetry Month will help. The circulation figures may show you need many more books on certain nonfiction topics, such as ancient Egypt, due to curriculum needs in the local school.

The physical condition of the materials should also be evaluated. If books look worn and tattered from use, it may be time to order replacement copies. Books that are repaired with noticeable tape may not continue to circulate as well; invest in a new copy if the book is in print. A new case on a CD or video/DVD will attract users. If a book is old but still looks new, it is a shelf sitter and is due to be weeded.

Children's Catalog, 18th ed., by Anne Price and Juliette Yaakov (New York H.W. Wilson, 2001), is the first resource librarians use for collection evaluation. This lists the books nearly every library should have in its children's department, and the titles are arranged by Dewey Decimal number. If you are new to your library, you may want to check these listings against the books on your shelves to see if you are missing any major areas.

WEEDING

Weeding, or "deselection," is the process of getting rid of books that are no longer popular, or that may be dated in such a way as to be inaccurate or even offensive. Keeping old, unpopular, inaccurate books just wastes shelf space, and it can be detrimental. Children may borrow books for a country report but find the outdated book lists a flag that is no longer used; even the name of the country may have changed! Old books on science experiments may offer projects that use harmful chemicals, or only feature white males in the photos of students doing the experiments. This sends the message that girls or nonwhite children are not interested in science.

It is fairly easy to weed books that are falling apart, or books that haven't been checked out in two years. It can be more difficult to determine which books are outdated and are inaccurate. A great Web site that offers monthly updates on topics for library weeding is http://www.sunlink. ucf.edu/weed/. Part of the state of Florida's school media resource Web site, this Web page offers a great overview of library weeding, as well as monthly topics on which to focus. For example, on the topic of weeding dinosaur books, it explains outdated names like brontosaurus; the accurate name is Apatosaurus, and your books should reflect this. Another helpful Web site is http://www.tsl.state.tx.us/ld/pubs/crew/toc.html, which is run by the Texas State Library. The site uses a method called CREW, which stands for Continuous Review, Evaluation, and Weeding. Although this Web site covers all library materials, it does have a special section on children's books and gives very clear instructions on weeding.

COLLECTION DEVELOPMENT

Now that you have evaluated and weeded the collection, it is time to start purchasing new materials and building the collection. What you purchase can differ greatly depending on whether you are at a school or a public library. School libraries need to offer books that the teachers assign; public libraries also need the books teachers assign, but usually they have larger budgets and can afford much more recreational reading, including paperback series fiction and media. When a school is using a reading promotional program such as Accelerated Reader or Scholastic Reading Counts! (SRC), school libraries will want titles on those lists. At a public library, your clientele will also want the recreational reading materials found on those lists. Although a public library serves a wider variety of public and private schools that don't all use a reading incentive program, you may have some of the titles, since your public library offers a wider variety of popular reading materials.

HOMEWORK-RELATED MATERIAL

Even though you are working at a public library, you should try to meet with teachers to see what books their students will be seeking at the library. This can be challenging for those in the public library sector, but it is not impossible. Maybe a phone call or e-mail is all that is needed to obtain assignments or reading lists. Many teachers will be happy to share that information, and since it is likely that other teachers of that grade level will be assigning the same books and topics, you only need input from a few teachers. Also, just helping students on a day-to-day basis, you will be asked for certain topics repeatedly, so you will know that those are popular subjects and may want to purchase new materials. Some librarians use "assignment alert cards," on which teachers let the library know about upcoming assignment topics. These are not used very frequently, however, so a quick phone call or e-mail to a friendly teacher can help you find out which books to purchase to help the students with homework assignments.

POPULARITY VERSUS QUALITY?

A big question in times of limited library budgets is whether you can afford popular materials or only have to spend your few dollars on quality materials. First, those two concepts are not mutually exclusive; some very popular books, such as J. K. Rowlings's <u>Harry Potter</u> series, are well written. Certain other popular series, for example R. L. Stein's <u>Goosebumps</u>, may not be as original but are very popular. Not purchasing them seems unfair to children; adults can check out similar popular fare like Danielle Steele novels at the library, so why can't children find popular material too? In the past, some libraries did not carry <u>Nancy Drew</u> books, or the <u>Oz</u> series, since some librarians did not find them of high literary quality; this attitude can lead to the library being seen as an elitist institution with no relevance to customer needs. Unless a library is on such a limited budget that it can only afford books related to the curriculum, some popular reading should be purchased. Series fiction, comic books, or magazines on music celebrities may bring in new library users if you carry what your audience wants.

TYPES OF MATERIALS

Libraries are not just for books anymore. If you are at a very small school library, you might not carry media for children to check out if your budget is very limited; however, when you are at a public library, offering media is now considered an essential service. Let's look at a quick overview of the types of materials most libraries carry for children to borrow. These include books, reference books, magazines, and parent and teacher resources.

Books

Books are still the largest category that libraries carry. In the children's department, you should have board books for babies, picture books, easy readers, transitional fiction, fiction, informational/nonfiction, picture books for older readers, and graphic novels. For more information about the different types of children's books, see chapter 3.

Reference Books

With the advent of the Internet, many libraries have reduced the number of reference books they carry. Having the *World Book Encyclopedia* on hand is essential; if all the computer terminals are in use, children can still find something on a topic. You can make a photocopy about this topic for the student even if all the books on the subject are out. An atlas, almanac, dictionary, and thesaurus are still helpful to have in hard copies.

Magazines

Magazines are a great way to get a "nonreader" to read. Many children who don't like to read chapter books will sit and read *Disney Adventures* or *Nickelodeon* magazine since these feature characters and actors from their favorite movies and television shows. *Sports Illustrated for Kids* features great color photos and interesting articles on sports stars and has clearly made an effort to include female athletes on a regular basis. Some public libraries find that video gaming magazines can be one of the most popular items in the library; these change quickly, so ask other librarians what they recommend. Some of these are not recommended for children due to the exploitative pictures of women.

Parent and Teacher Resources

In a public library, there may be many parents and teachers using the children's area. See if you can set up a special shelf of newer items that will appeal to them. Often a parent is "stuck" in the children's room while the kids play on the computer or do homework; if you have materials on child behavior the parents will have something to read while they wait. The same is true for teachers; a teacher may come by to get a read-aloud copy of the latest Newbery winner, so offer him or her a shelf of teacher resource books with creative ideas on teaching art, poetry, or other topics.

MEDIA

In a public library, having media for patrons to check out can attract customers who don't think of themselves as readers. If you have free DVDs right near the picture books, parents may come in for the latest children's film and leave with a stack of books, too. Media can also be helpful to children with learning disabilities, especially books on tape or CD. The child can listen to the story being read out loud on the tape and follow along with the book.

Music CDs

Music has been proven to help brain development in babies and young children, plus it is fun! Children's music CDs can be a great resource for preschool teachers and daycare providers, as well as parents who drive children to practices or during commuting and trips. You can also use music CDs in your library storytimes.

CD-ROMs

Educational CD-ROMs can assist children in learning math, spelling, reading, and other subjects. Most now are compatible with both PCs and Macs, and they can also help children who are learning English. Most librarians find there are plenty of CD-ROMs that combine fun with learning, so you do not have to feel compelled to carry video game computer programs.

Video/DVD

Free videos and DVDs can get nonusers to use the library instead of the local video store. Many kids' movies are based on children's books and are even used in classrooms. These can greatly increase a library's circulation figures, and some are useful to teachers, who can tie them into the science or social studies areas of the curriculum. Children's DVDs cost the same as a hardback book; if you are not currently carrying them, give it a try. You will soon find some new customers who may come for the DVDs but will leave with books, too.

Recorded Books

Whether a novel on CD or tape, or a picture book and tape together, recorded books are growing in popularity. They are a life saver for children who are learning English or who have a learning disability like dyslexia, who use them to facilitate reading assignments. They are also useful for parents who want something fun and educational to listen to on car trips. The unabridged versions are always preferable, especially if the child is going to read along with the text.

PURCHASING RECOMMENDATIONS

Most librarians keep up with what is new and recommended by reading book review journals such as *School Library Journal* or *Horn Book Magazine.* Another practical way to know what to purchase is to look at lists of award winners including the Newbery and Caldecott awards and the Coretta Scott King awards, and "best books" lists such as the Notable Children's Books list from the American Library Association's (ALA) division, the Association of Library Service to Children (ALSC). To find nonfiction series that will help students working on reports, many librarians will look at book catalogs and meet with salespeople from different publishers. For media, there are also catalogs and special Web sites that offer educational videos and DVDs as well as CD-ROMs.

Review Journals

Journals that review children's books and media are an essential resource for children's librarians. Even though it is called *School Library Journal*, public libraries will find this magazine as useful as school librarians do. Besides reviewing books and media, it has lots of great articles each month on library programming, trends, author interviews, technology, and more. Its reviews are written by a wide variety of volunteers who are children's librarians, and its media reviews are very extensive, helping librarians know whether a media item is good for classroom use. *Booklist* has reviews of books and media for all ages (adults included) and often lists children's books in a series. *Horn Book* is a more literary review guide and usually only lists books it is endorsing. It also has great articles on children's literature. *Publishers Weekly* is aimed more at bookstore owners, but many librarians appreciate the children's section, which reviews books most likely to be best sellers, and it is one of the few journals that reviews board books, popup and toy books, and popular children's series.

Awards/Bests Lists

Even if a library has a very limited budget, it is likely to want to purchase the major children's book award winners. This would include the Newbery Medal and Honor books, the Caldecott Medal and Honor books, the Coretta Scott King Award for best African American children's books, the Pura Belpre Award for the best Latino/Hispanic children's books, and the Sibert Award for the best informational children's books. These are all administered by divisions of ALA, and the lists can be found at www.ala.org/ala/alsc/awardsscholarships/literaryawds/literaryrelated.htm. The ALSC also posts annual Notables lists: of notable children's books, children's audio recordings, and children's video and DVD. Each state also has its own awards; check out your state's library association website for information. But before we move on, let's find out a little more about the national awards.

No book award has more influence on sales than the Newbery Medal, not the National Book Award, the Pulitzer, or even the Caldecott; for Newbery winners don't go out of print, are almost always found on the shelf of even the smallest library, and are impervious to book-banners and book-burners in even the most conservative communities. Just what are these awards, and who gets to pick?

The Newbery Award, instituted in 1922, and the Caldecott Award, begun in 1937, are both administered by ALSC. For a long time, one yearly appointed committee had to choose both the Newbery and Caldecott awards. Since about thirty years ago, two committees have met, one for each award. The committee members are like jurors; they are not paid, they meet in private, and their deliberations and debates are not recorded or divulged. Committee members must be ALSC/ALA members; about half are elected and the other half are appointed, and they serve for just one year. They may serve again after a five-year break.

The Newbery is given to the author of the "most distinguished contribution to American literature for children." It goes to a book for the writing, not the illustrations, and not for popularity, nor for how the book will fit into school curriculum. It does have to go to an American, which is why Roald Dahl never won, and why J. K. Rowling is not eligible.

The Caldecott Award was devised to award an artist for "the most distinguished American picture book for children." For the Caldecott Medal, the award is for the artwork, so if the text is a little "ordinary," that doesn't matter. If the text is downright bad, or inaccurate, the committee can take that into consideration, because the award considers "the excellence of pictorial interpretation of the story," meaning, if the story is really bad, it won't matter if the pictures are beautiful.

Both committees have always chosen "Honor" Books for both the Newbery and Caldecott. For about the past thirty years, there has been a limit of five Honor books (although a committee doesn't have to name five, they just can't name more than five). In 2004, *Crispin: Cross of Lead* by Avi won, and five Honor books were named. If you read all six, they are all fiction aimed at middle schoolers, although nonfiction is eligible and books for younger readers are also eligible. It's interesting that most winners and honor books seem to fit the middle school fiction (grades six to eight) category.

Laura Ingalls Wilder, author of the Little House series of pioneer stories, was a five-time Newbery Honor recipient, but never a Newbery Medalist. So ALA named an award just for her, and she was its first recipient. The Laura Ingalls Wilder Award goes to an author or illustrator for his or her body of work; recipients have included Beverly Cleary, Dr. Seuss, and nonfiction author Milton Meltzer. It is considered a lifetime achievement award. To find out more about the Newbery, Caldecott, and Wilder awards, visit www.ala.org.

In 1975, Virginia Hamilton was awarded the Newbery for *M.C. Higgins the Great,* and in 1977, Mildred Taylor won for *Roll of Thunder, Hear My Cry.* But previously, in 1969, African American and other librarians who were tired of waiting for some acknowledgment of the contributions of African American authors and illustrators to children's literature started the Coretta Scott King Awards, with criteria similar to those for the Newbery and Caldecott, but to award excellence in children's literature by African Americans. In 1999, *Bud Not Buddy* by Christopher Paul Curtis was the first children's book to receive both the Newbery Medal and Coretta Scott King Award; ironically, the announcement of the awards took place on the Monday morning of the Dr. Martin Luther King Jr. holiday! The Coretta Scott King Awards are administered by the Social Responsibilities Round Table (SRRT) of ALA.

In just the past few years, a new ALA/ALSC award has been given, the Sibert, awarded to the best informational book for children. The Young Adult Library Services Association (YALSA), the ALA division for young adult librarians, recently started the Prinze Award, similar to the Newbery although the authors do not have to be American, for the best young adult book. For a long time, the National Book Award stopped giving an award for its "Youth" category, but that was reinstated a few years ago. So there is a plethora of awards! These awards can be a starting point if you are new at purchasing children's books for your library.

Catalogs

Sometimes the most useful books for homework assignments are series nonfiction books. Look at children's book catalogs from various publishers to see what they have listed. Take the time to meet with the salespeople who come to your library to show you samples. Many book salespeople are former teachers and know what will work in the classroom and for assignments, and what may be better for recreational summer reading. Book salespeople want repeat customers, so they will let you know if something isn't the best for your students and what is a better alternative for your customers.

Media Recommendations

Media can be more difficult to find for classroom use than books. Reviews in *School Library Journal* are very helpful. Also try www.libraryvideo.com for media; the site has a very useful online catalog. You can search it by subject, if you are looking for media on a certain topic. For popular movies, try www.midwesttapes.com, which lists popular mainstream video and DVD and has a great children's movie area.

Vendors' Web Sites

Book Wholesalers, Inc. (www.bwibooks.com) started by only carrying children's books for libraries; they have expanded and now sell adult books and media. You have to register to use their Web site, but it is free, and most public librarians use BWI as their children's books vendor. They list the professional reviews for each book, and have great subject lists.

Titlewave (www.titlewave.com) is the online catalog of Follett, which is a major children's bookseller for school libraries. It is similar to BWI in what is offered, and although you have to register to use the site, it is free.

Non-English Materials

Besides the regular children's book vendors listed above who sell books in Spanish and other languages besides English, there are some other resources for finding books in foreign languages. Here are some useful Web sites:

www.csusm.edu/csb. This is the Web site for Barahona Center for Books in Spanish for Children and Adolescents, at California State University, San Marcos. It lists recommended children's books in Spanish or bilingual Spanish/English books.

http://www.shens.com/. Shen's is a children's book distribution company that specializes in children's multicultural books in English and children's books in other languages, including Spanish, and Asian languages such as Chinese, Japanese, and Vietnamese.

http://www.lectorum.com/. Lectorum is part of Scholastic Books, and distributes over 25,000 different children's titles in Spanish, as well as bilingual books in English and Spanish.

BOOK SELECTION: MORE THAN SHOPPING

Book selection can be a favorite task of children's librarians; after all, it involves getting to spend someone else's money on books and media! Of course, it is a great responsibility too, and since most librarians have such limited budgets, we need to spend very wisely. With the Internet, it can be easier than it used to be to search for books on specific topics, using vendor Web sites like www.bwibooks.com. The professional reviews are often listed on the Web site, so you can confirm you are buying something recommended by other librarians. These reviews can be very helpful when someone brings you a "challenge" on a particular book. It may be a parent objecting to a book the library has purchased, or you may be targeted by a particular group wishing to remove certain books from all libraries. You can use the reviews to show that the book was highly recommended and for what age group, and that the reviews were written for school and public children's librarians to use as a tool to purchase appropriate materials. Book selection doesn't mean you are a censor, but the reviews allow you to decide whether an item is better for the children's room or the Young Adult area, for example. Book selection is an ongoing part of a children's librarian's job, because curriculum changes and books become dated. Also, trends in recreational reading change very quickly, and book selection is very important to keep children coming to the library for books they want to read for fun. Now, if only the budgets could increase!

Chapter 5

Storytime

WHAT IS STORYTIME?

Storytimes have been in libraries for more than a hundred years, and they are still a vital and essential service. Sometimes these programs are referred to as "story hour," even if they last thirty minutes. This chapter covers the "how to" of doing storytimes for babies, toddlers, preschoolers, and families, to make them fun and exciting, and to assist parents in getting their children ready for kindergarten. Staff will discover that storytime doesn't require one to play the guitar or "perform," but rather to choose entertaining books and present them in a comfortable manner. Props, storytelling, puppets, and crafts are covered, as well as publicity and making storytime accessible to a wide audience by reducing red tape. While parents are attending or bringing their children to storytime, you will have an opportunity to talk with them about reading to their children. If you provide a "parents' bookshelf," you can point out its location and they can look there while their children are listening.

WHY WE DO STORYTIME

Storytime was the first library "program," and we do storytime because it introduces preschoolers to good books and conveys the idea that books and reading are valuable. It also models read-aloud techniques for the parents who attend, boosts circulation, and helps preschoolers get ready for kindergarten. They learn skills such as listening to the teacher, sitting quietly, and paying attention. Reading specialists have determined that the one constant in creating a successful reader is a child who is read to on a regular daily basis. Reading ability isn't based on income or class, but on the fact that someone read to that child on a daily basis. When parents start coming to storytime, they quickly learn that the public library is a major parenting resource center. A big bonus is that the family gets in the habit of coming to the library. When they become regular library users, even as the children grow older, the family will keep coming back for other programming, homework resources, and media.

REGISTRATION OR NOT?

Libraries traditionally have done "preschool storytimes" aimed at those three to five years of age. The library took signups that limited a storytime to twenty-five children. Many librarians still require registration for their storytimes, so do some research and decide what will be best for your community. Those who serve adult learners in literacy programs urge libraries to avoid registration for storytime, since that acts as a barrier to the adult learners. Since that particular audience can greatly gain from attending storytime, accommodating them should be a top priority.

Many libraries have expanded, and now have a baby storytime (sometimes called Lapsit or Baby Bounce), a toddler storytime, a preschool storytime, and an evening family storytime that is for all ages. Many libraries have eliminated registration for storytime. This helps those parents with limited English or with literacy needs, because there are no barriers to attending a storytime.

In the past, parents weren't allowed in the storytime room, but now they are encouraged to attend because they act as ushers, and they benefit from seeing a storytime modeled. Some librarians think parents talk too much during storytime. If this happens, just ask them to stop!

FORMATS BY AGE: LAPSIT, TODDLER, PRESCHOOL

Storytime is not done just one way; in fact, many libraries will have bilingual storytimes, and many but not all include craft projects. Some people do not do themed storytimes, while many librarians feel more comfortable doing themes; you have to do what is right for you. Themes would include having the stories and craft project, but not necessarily the songs, be on the same topic: dogs, Halloween, the alphabet, firefighters, dinosaurs, and so forth. Storytimes usually feature twenty-five to thirty minutes of the songs and books, with the preschool storytime allowing fifteen to twenty-five minutes for the craft or art project at the end. For lapsit and toddler time, crafts are usually not included, since that age group isn't developmentally ready for crafts; the kids cannot hold crayons or use scissors yet. But you can end toddler time or lapsit with a song, or a dance, or by stamping the child's hand with creative rubber stamps found at teacher supply stores. Some libraries conclude their lapsit by handing out board books for each parent and baby to read together; then it is up to the parents if they want to check out the board book or put it back in the basket. Some toddler times conclude with an activity song, like the "Hokey Pokey" or other movement song. Then everyone is up on their feet and ready to go look at books or head to the circulation desk. Since the lapsit and toddler storytimes involve so many songs, three or four at least in each session, and you will want to repeat songs, you may want to make handouts of the lyrics for parents. Many parents did not grow up in the United States, and may not know common songs like "Head and Shoulders, Knees and Toes," so the lyric sheets can be a great help.

STORYTIME FORMAT

Just to review, a common storytime would include the following:

1. Opening song: "Hello Everybody, Yes Indeed" or "Wheels on the Bus."

2. Stating the theme: "We are going to hear some stories about the library."

3. Read *D.W.'s Library Card* by Marc Brown.

4. Song: "Head and Shoulders, Knees and Toes."

5.   Read *I Took My Frog to the Library* by Eric Kimmel.

6.   Sing "Five Green and Speckled Frogs."

7.   Read *Tiny Goes to the Library* by Cari Meister.

8.   Sing "Eency Weensy Spider."

9.   Read *I Like Books* by Anthony Browne.

10.   Sing "Wheels On the Bus" and conclude storytime.

11.   Stamp each child's hand with a rubber stamp and special safe ink, or, for older kids who can do a craft, make a bookmark or an Arthur or D.W. mask (found at http://pbskids.org/arthur/).

Now that we are all on the same page about what a storytime encompasses, let's look at some common questions regarding storytimes, and some ways to "jazz up" a storytime, so even the most wiggling toddler will enjoy it. But if you are still unclear on the format of storytime, be sure to visit another library where you can observe one in person; there is no substitute for actually seeing a storytime where parents and children are together.

PHYSICAL ENVIRONMENT

Whether holding the storytime in a meeting room or in the children's area of the library itself, some basic "rules" of the physical area will work to your advantage. Preschoolers can sit in a semicircle on the carpet, facing the staff member, with parents sitting toward the back of the circle. Some parents like to hold their child on their lap (which is fine!); that works if they sit toward the back or sides of the circle so they are not blocking anyone's view. Some parents like to sit in a chair at the back and let their children sit on the carpet by themselves. That is fine too; many grandparents or older caregivers and expectant moms find sitting on the floor uncomfortable. It is not recommended that the children sit in chairs; the carpet works better and you can fit more people. If the floor is not carpeted, see if a local store will donate old carpet sample squares, or have the Friends of the Library purchase a children's carpet, available at teacher supply stores (such as www.lakeshorelearning.com).

Think of the area where the reader sits as the "stage": You want to be a little higher than the audience, who are on the floor, so you will probably want a chair or small stool to sit on. Try not to have anything distracting behind you, like a walking area, window, or clock; sit against a blank wall if possible. Try to sit with the entrance door to the back of the circle; that way, latecomers won't distract the audience because the door is not in the line of sight of the audience. The reader should hold the book with the page facing the audience; do this by grasping the lower edge of the book, with the book's open spine in your hand to hold it open. That way, you can see the book and the audience can as well. Slowly pass the book in front of you from one side to the other, so everyone can see. Turn the page and read, then pass again to the other side.

PREPARATION

Just how much time does it take to prepare for storytime? That depends on how much time you have. If you wear many hats and don't have a lot of preparation time, try to read the book to yourself at least three times; that should be sufficient to have a natural rhythm to your reading. That will be especially helpful with rhyming books, so you can anticipate the beat of the lines of poetry. If you repeat songs, that will also decrease how much preparation time you need. Learning a new song every week is a luxury that few of us can afford, but if you have time, great! But children like songs to be repeated more often than stories, so learning five or six songs to begin with is plenty. Then you can add a new song approximately once a month.

The craft project (if you include one) should take very little prep. Maybe just photocopy the coloring sheet or cut outs; if it takes more time than that, see if teen volunteers can do the preparation for you. Most high school students are now required to do volunteer service to graduate, and they can be a great help in preparing craft projects that need pre-gluing or pre-cutting.

SCHEDULING

The scheduling of the different types of storytimes will depend on the target audience; it is important that the time of day be convenient for the parent and child, and not at naptime, for example. Of course, you want to schedule the storytimes when it is convenient for staff, but not if it is a time when no one will attend!

Lapsit

Mornings are usually the best time to engage children under the age of five or six. They are awake and not yet ready for naptime; they have had breakfast and are not yet hungry for lunch. Try holding the lapsit/baby storytime, for infants age six to eighteen months, even before the library opens. If the library opens at 10:00 A.M., begin Lapsit at 9:30 A.M., so by the time you have concluded the storytime, the library is open and parents can check out books. The mornings seem to work best as the babies are not as sleepy or cranky.

Toddler Time

Toddlers range from age twelve months to three years of age, so there is some overlap with lapsit and preschool storytimes. Toddler time can be held at 11:00 A.M. on the same day as the lapsit. Some families stay for both because they have a baby and a toddler. The toddler time runs about twenty-five minutes. That time seems to work really well; it isn't nap time, and you can conclude in plenty of time for them to get back home for lunch.

Preschool Storytime

Many libraries will hold two sessions of preschool storytime, which use the same books, on the same day: one at 10:30 A.M. and one at 1:30 P.M., for example. The afternoon storytime attracts many kindergartners and older preschoolers (four-year-olds) who no longer take naps. The morning session seems to attract more young preschoolers who do take naps. You can also hold an evening family storytime, which attracts babies, toddlers, preschoolers, and kids in kindergarten and first through third grades. It is attended by families whose work schedules prevent them from coming to the other storytimes. Depending on your area, the evening storytime can begin at 7:00 P.M. or 7:30 P.M. Try the earlier time, and if most folks come late, or if you get little turnout, try the later time. If you live in an area where many working parents have a long commute, the later time will be better.

GETTING STARTED

If you will be starting up storytime at your library, either for the first time or after a period without any, start with a weekly preschool storytime in the morning. If that is well attended, branch out to an evening storytime for working parents. If you are in a suburban area, this is very likely to be well attended if the word gets out that it is being held. At a downtown city library, evening storytimes may not meet much need unless there is a lot of housing in the area; if it is all office buildings, having an evening storytime at a branch library nearer to family housing may be more popular. If both the morning preschool storytime and the evening family storytime grow to be well attended, add a lapsit on a different morning. Then expand to a toddler time if that will meet a need. This will take time; you may want to add a new storytime just once a year, especially if you are the only full-time staff member.

Some libraries schedule their storytime sessions like college classes; the sessions may last eight to ten weeks, then there is a break. For some of the families who attend, that can be confusing. Holding storytimes on a more regular basis is easier for parents and caregivers to remember, especially if you don't have registration, and if you want to include more families still learning English. It is easier to remember that storytime is every Tuesday morning at 10:30 A.M. than to remember what eight-week period is set aside for storytime sessions.

OUTREACH

If you aren't getting a good attendance at your storytime, try doing it in the evening, or on Saturdays; there are more children in daycare and fewer stay at home moms to attend morning storytimes in some areas. Find out what works best for your community. You can also have flyers available at local pediatricians' offices, churches and other houses of worship, stores that specialize in merchandise for infants and young children, and any other place where parents of young children may go on a regular basis. Also, see if your local paper can do a feature on storytime or run a photo and a short announcement informing the community about the library's storytime.

RESEARCH

Much research has been conducted on early brain development, especially in the past few years, and there has been a lot of media coverage on this. Stories in *Time* and other magazines, newspapers, and the TV news are telling parents that even babies need to be read to. It shouldn't be too difficult to find some of these articles if you need justification for having lapsit or toddler time in a written proposal for starting these storytimes. Pediatricians are also helping to promote reading to infants and young children with a program called "Reach Out and Read." In this program, doctors give a free book to a child when the child comes for his or her "well baby" visit, which they do about every six months. This includes visits where they get their inoculations and tests for hearing and other developmental testing. The doctors give out free books and remind parents how important it is to read to a child. If you have flyers available about your storytimes, doctors may distribute them for you.

STORYTELLING OR STORYTIME?

Storytelling means the performance of stories by a storyteller, who has memorized the story and doesn't refer to the book to tell the story. It is an actor's craft. It's like doing a monologue. On the other hand, storytime (or story hour) usually involves the use of picture books to share stories, along with songs, fingerplays, maybe a dance like "The Hokey Pokey," or maybe an art or craft project at the end. Some librarians do add one short, memorized story to a storytime, one that doesn't involve holding up a book, and that is a nice bonus. If you want to find out more about the art of storytelling, look for any of the storytelling books mentioned later in this chapter. But don't feel obligated to learn storytelling unless you have time and the desire; your storytimes can be successful without doing performance storytelling.

SONGS: AN ESSENTIAL PART

The format of storytime can vary, but the format we used in the "Library" themed storytime mentioned earlier is pretty common. I try to keep the welcome song and the closing song the same each time. I also try to do a song in between each book, like "Open, Shut Them"; a fingerplay like "Five Little Monkeys Jumping on the Bed"; or "Shake Your Hands." These songs signal the kids that it is time to "criss-cross applesauce" and listen. I actually do the same songs over and over, even if they don't fit the theme, whereas other librarians may introduce more songs and repeat them far less often. If you don't know what songs to use, watch *Barney,* a PBS television series, which uses most of the songs already mentioned, because the songs they use are in the public domain. Another way to learn storytime songs is to watch a Raffi video, or a Bev Bos video; many of the parents and children will know the songs featured on these videos.

CHOOSING PICTURE BOOKS

Picture books should be chosen according to the age of the children in your storytime. Children who have just turned three won't sit still for the same story that a five-year-old can sit through. Several reference books are available to help you choose books for storytime; they are listed at the end of this chapter. I also try to have at least one interactive, or participatory, story at each storytime, which I cover below. One rule of thumb is to find picture books with just one or two sentences per page. If a book has a paragraph on each page, it may be better suited to kinder-gartners and first-grade read-alouds than to a preschool storytime.

DIFFERENT TYPES OF STORIES

Now let's cover the different types of interactive or participatory stories that can jazz up your storytimes: cumulative, circular stories, par-ticipation stories, concept books, creative dramatics, and songs and fingerplays.

Cumulative

Cumulative stories are like *The House That Jack Built* by Simms Taback, which have reoccurring phrases that are added on, so the listener can chant along. Two excellent new books are *The Chair Where Bear Sits* by Lee Wardlow and *The Jacket I Wear in the Snow* by Shirley Neitzel. The Neitzel book has the added element of the rebus.

Circular Stories

Circular stories end up where they started. One of the most popular is *If You Give a Mouse a Cookie* by Laura Numeroff, and you may have seen her follow-up books, *If You Give a Pig a Pancake* and *If You Give a Mouse a Muffin.* Circular stories offer listeners the opportunity to predict what will happen in the story, a skill they will need in kindergarten.

Participation Stories

Often called repetitive stories, pattern stories, or call and response stories, these are stories where the listener calls out a repeated phrase. A great example is *The Little Red Hen* by Byron Barton, where listeners call out "Not I!" whenever one of the characters says "Not I!" I try to do at least one participatory story during each storytime. Try *Mama Cat Has Three Kittens* by Denise Fleming or *Fortunately* by Remy Charlip. You may already know *Go Away, Big Green Monster* by Ed Emberley, and one of my new favorites is *What Shall We Do With the Boo-Hoo Baby?* by Cressida Cowell. Also look for any books by Margaret Read MacDonald, like *Fat Cat: A Danish Folktale* and *Mabela the Clever.* Any book with a repeated phrase can be made interactive. One of the most popular is *Brown Bear, Brown Bear, What Do You See?* by Bill Martin.

Concept Books

Alphabet and counting books are easy to make call and response, because the audience can yell out the letter or number on that page of the book. Also, books about shapes, opposites, or colors can invite interaction, with the audience guessing the example of the concept shown in that part of the story. Some of the best concept books actually have a plot, like *Miss Bindergarten Gets Ready for Kindergarten* by Joseph Slate or *Feast for Ten* by Cathryn Falwell.

Creative Dramatics

A creative dramatic story is one that can be acted out. These books are found less often than cumulative or participatory stories, but they can be very successful at energizing a storytime. One of the most popular is *We're Going on a Bear Hunt* by Michael Rosen. A new version of this old story is *We're Going on a Ghost Hunt* by Marcia Vaughan. Another old favorite is the Russian folktale *The Enormous Turnip* by Alexis Tolstoy, where kids are selected to play the farmer, the dog, the cat, and the bird, who try to pull up the gigantic turnip. A variation that is popular at Halloween is *The Big Pumpkin* by Erica Silverman. Another easy creative dramatic story is *Wiggle Waggle* by Jonathan London.

Songs and Fingerplays

You don't need to play the guitar or be a good singer to include songs in your storytime. You don't have to speak a foreign language to include multicultural songs or fingerplays, either. You can find many CDs and videos with children's songs that you can learn from, and lots of picture books that are based on songs. These can include *Who Took the Cookies from the Cookie Jar?* by Jane Manning; *Earthsong* by Sally Rogers which is a variation on "Over in the Meadow"; *The Itsy Bitsy Spider* by Iza Trapani; *Old MacDonald Had a Farm* by Pam Adams; and *The Balancing Act* by Merle Peek, which is the English version of a song also popular in Spanish, "Un Elefante." A good Web site source is www.kididdles.com/mouseum, which allows you to hear the song and to print out the lyrics.

Many books are available with fingerplays, including *My First Action Rhymes* by Lynne Cravath and Joanna Cole's *The Eentsy Weentsy Spider: Fingerplays and Action Rhymes.* You can also find individual picture books based on fingerplays, such as *Peanut Butter and Jelly* by Nadine Bernard Westcott and *Five Little Monkeys Sitting in a Tree* by Eileen Christelow. For multicultural fingerplays, try *Chinese Mother Goose Rhymes* by Robert Wyndham or *Diez Deditos: Ten Little Fingers* by Jose Luis Orozco. A good Web site resource for fingerplays is http://falcon.jmu.edu/~ramseyil/fingerplayindex.htm.

BOOKS FOR VERY YOUNG CHILDREN

Don't forget board books. Even though they are small in size and won't carry if you have a big audience, they will work for groups of fifteen pairs (fifteen babies and fifteen parents) or fewer at a lapsit storytime. Following are board books to consider:

The Bear Went Over the Mountain by Rosemary Wells

You Are My Perfect Baby by Joyce Carol Thomas

Julius's Candy Corn by Kevin Henkes

Often board books will be a revised edition that was originally a picture book, and that may mean it is abridged (but not always). Skip these, and just use board books that started out as board books. And don't forget that you might ask parents to share a board book with their babies at the close of a lapsit program.

SHORT PICTURE BOOKS

You will have many choices for very brief picture books, such as the following, with bright, clear, not too detailed illustrations that have been big hits at lapsit and toddler time:

My Two Hands/My Two Feet by Rick Walton

The Three Bears by Byron Barton

Chicka Chicka Boom Boom by Bill Martin, Jr and John Archambault

Time for Bed by Mem Fox

This Is the Farmer by Nancy Tafuri

Vroomaloom Zoom by John Coy

Crunch Munch by Jonathan London

Another Important Book by Margaret Wise Brown

Baby Rock, Baby Roll by Stella Blackstone

Also, look for other books by these same authors. You will find more that are great for storytime for the very young, along with books by Eric Carle and others.

BIG BOOKS

About 100 big books are available in print from several publishers. These are oversized versions of regular picture books, about two feet by three feet (poster sized) paperback versions of popular picture books such as *Madeline* by Ludwig Bemelmans. One vendor that carries many of these is Lakeshore Teacher's Store, which has a Web site you can order from, www.lakeshorelearning.com, as well as a catalog. These can be really helpful if you find your storytimes have a large turnout and you are concerned that the kids cannot see the pictures in regular-sized books.

GAMES

Games can be a special feature of a storytime every once in a while. In toddler time, we often do a circle game or dance, like "The Hokey Pokey," or "Farmer in the Dell." Other simple games include "Duck, Duck, Goose," or "Simon Says." Games are a great way to hold the audience's attention if they are having an extra wiggling day.

PUPPETS

A puppet can be a great way to start off storytime. It can become the signal that storytime is starting. You can also get puppets that go with a certain book, like *Go Away, Big Green Monster* by Ed Emberley, or apron figures, like those that go with *The Napping House* by Audrey Wood and Don Wood. These are also available at the Lakeshore teacher's store mentioned above. Folkmanis is a great company that makes and sells realistic looking animal puppets; see the Web site at www.folkmanis.com.

FLANNELBOARDS

Flannelboards are still very popular, even though librarians have been using them for storytimes since the 1930s or even earlier! Basically, they are cut out felt figures that attach to an upright board covered in flannel. These can be helpful in telling a story to a large group, when the picture book would be too small to be seen by those in the back of the room. For more on flannelboards, visit www.sisters-in-stitches.com.

KINDERGARTEN READINESS

To increase attendance at your storytime, the library should emphasize to parents that preschool storytime offers kindergarten readiness; print it on the flyers since it seems to help motivate parents to attend. If you want to increase your storytime attendance, this is a great way to convince parents that storytime is worth their time. As you may know, children entering kindergarten are often given a "readiness" exam: Can they use scissors, write their names, or say their telephone numbers? Of course, being read to is one of the most important parts of kindergarten readiness, but the craft activities cover some of the parts of that readiness test (do you know your colors, can you hold a crayon properly?), and parents may need to learn about kindergarten readiness to encourage them to fit storytime into their busy schedules. If you need more information about kindergarten readiness, talk to a local kindergarten teacher to see what the standards are in your area. But don't be surprised if kindergarten sounds more like what you did in first grade; kindergarten often includes much more reading and writing then it did twenty years ago, so preschoolers need more kindergarten readiness skills than they did previously. Storytime can help communicate these changes, since many parents of preschoolers may be unaware of how much is asked of a child entering school.

ARTS AND CRAFTS

Arts and crafts are a new element to library storytimes; you will find that ending with a simple craft project is a great way to attract new audience members and add elements of kindergarten readiness, plus it can be fun! A craft project can reinforce the theme of the storytime and let children practice scissor skills and coloring, which are part of kindergarten readiness. The important thing to remember about arts and crafts is that "it is the process, not the product" that matters. The children get more out of doing it themselves than if it looks like Martha Stewart (or the parent) did the project. The crafts should be very inexpensive and shouldn't take a lot of preparation time. Most of the time, crafts are just photocopied handouts that get cut and colored, and maybe are glued on a popsicle stick or made into a paper bag puppet. Many Web sites are available on arts and crafts projects, such as www.craftsforkids.com or www.enchantedlearning.com. I try to choose the craft to go with the stories, not the other way around. The craft is an extra, not the reason for storytime, but it can really make for a great conclusion to the storytime. The item acts like a souvenir to remind kids of the stories that were read that day.

BEHAVIOR

New storytime readers often are concerned about having a child who won't sit still, or one that won't listen during the storytime. Don't worry too much if the younger babies and toddlers don't seem to be paying attention; you will be surprised how much they will retain. For example, even if a toddler sits with his back to you, or is wandering around the perimeter, he will still remember much of what you said. So long as a child's behavior isn't hurting the experience for others, don't let it bother you. That doesn't mean you have to put up with noisy kids or talking parents, however. I often will ask, "Could the parent help me with this child, I am not sure everyone can hear (or see)?" That often will lead the parent to hold the child on his or her lap so the noise or distraction will stop, yet it doesn't embarrass the parent. I try to phrase things in a positive say so it doesn't come across as a list of "don'ts." For example, instead of a rule saying "No toys or food allowed," you could say "Save toys and snacks until after storytime because you need your hands free for the fingerplays." You may also have to state the obvious: "No cell phones" and "Stay in the library" are two rules parents need spelled out for them even though many of us would take those rules for granted. Also, singing a song between each story allows for latecomers to grab a seat, or for people to reposition themselves to a more comfortable seat.

Having a volunteer can also be a great help at storytime; he or she can usher latecomers to their seats or help with children who cannot find their caregivers.

BILINGUAL STORYTIMES

Many communities will find that doing a storytime in Spanish, or in Spanish and English, will serve a large portion of their residents. For ideas on bilingual storytimes, check out *25 Latino Craft Projects* by Ana Elba Pavon and Diana Borrego (Chicago: American Library Association, 2003). The authors are both children's librarians, and although the title doesn't indicate it, there is lots of advice on doing bilingual storytimes and other programs, and lots of book suggestions in this resource. Another great resource is the Web site www.bibliotecasparalagente.org, from the Northern California chapter of REFORMA, an ALA organization for library services to Spanish-speaking residents. Of course Spanish isn't the only language used in some areas; your community may benefit from a bilingual storytime in Vietnamese or Russian. See what the need is and go from there.

PREP INVOLVED IN YOUR STORYTIME

How much work should it be to prepare for storytime? That depends, but if you usually use the same songs over and over, learning songs doesn't take a lot of preparation. Read each story at least twice through to get the pacing and so forth, but you don't need to memorize the story. And if the craft takes more than photocopying a page, get a teen volunteer to cut out the projects, or make a sample. That way your preparation time will be fairly minimal.

ASSISTING PARENTS

When parents bring their children to the library, you are given a great opportunity to talk with them about reading to their children. It also provides you with an opportunity to suggest materials they may need to help them be good parents.

Allowing parents to participate in storytime is a great way to model read-aloud techniques for parents. It also allows parents to see the types of books you are choosing for young children, so they can conclude their visit by choosing similar books to take home and read at bedtime or other times. Having parents at storytime also gives you a contact with them, so later when they are finding homework or recreational reading books, they will remember when you were the storytime person and know you are a friendly face at the library.

Many public libraries now have a "parents' shelf" in the children's room. This area will have books on child development, behavior and discipline, baby names, traveling with children, decorating a child's room, and more. Some parents will bring their children to the library but never venture into the adult book area. If this is true, your parent's shelf can show them there are great books for them. The parents' shelf can also hold the interest of parents who must stay in the same room with their young children. They will now have something to read while their preschoolers are looking for picture books or playing a computer learning game.

Preschools and Daycares

More children are in preschool and daycare than are with "stay-at-home" moms: 60 percent of all preschoolers in the United States spend some of the work week in daycare. That means many three- and four-year-olds don't have a parent available to take them to pre-school storytime at the library. To serve those children, you can offer storytimes to daycare groups that can come to the library. Many daycares do not have transportation to take the children to the library; instead, the library can assist the providers who want to do the storytime at their sites by having specialized book bags to check out with lots of great picture books, crafts, and puppets. Offer daycare providers a once a year orientation on doing storytime at their site; it can be a one- or two-hour workshop on a Saturday morning. Offer refreshments, prizes, and other incentives to get the daycare providers to attend. Then they will find out what types of books are best for the young children in their care, and they will often become regular library users. If you think about it, one daycare provider checking out books represents several children who will be read to because of the outreach the library did to the daycare provider.

You can even go out to the preschool center to do storytime, although this can be labor intensive. An easier solution is to have an annual program for preschool teachers and daycare providers at which you show new picture books, craft ideas, and other resources the library can offer them to take to their students. It is a win-win situation!

RESOURCES FOR STORYTIME

You can find many great books filled with themes, booklists, crafts, and advice for running a storytime. These can be a great help when getting started and can also be inspirational for longtime storytime readers who need to freshen up their repertoire!

If you want to start a lapsit storytime for babies, an essential guide is *Literate Beginnings: Programs for Babies and Toddlers* by Debby Ann Jeffery (Chicago: American Library Association, 1995). Although it is out of print, see if you can find a used copy. Jeffery was a librarian at San Francisco Public Library and conducted very popular storytimes for babies, so her advice is based on practical experience as well as research. Her book contains lyrics to songs and is arranged by themes.

Two great books with ideas for toddler storytimes are *I'm a Little Teapot!* by Jane Cobb (Vancouver: BC: Black Sheep Press, 2001) and *Storytimes for Two Year Olds,* 2d ed., by Judy Nichols (Chicago: American Library Association, 1998). Filled with ideas to keep the attention of the "totally nonstop toddler," these list storytime themes along with related books, songs, fingerplays, and crafts for that theme.

A great book with a wealth of ideas for storytimes, general children's library programs, and storytelling is Caroline Feller Bauer's *New Handbook for Storytellers* (Chicago: American Library Association, 1995). You could try just one new idea a month from Bauer's book and not be finished for several years, she offers so many great ideas!

Librarian Connie Champlin's *Storytelling with Puppets,* 2d ed. (Chicago: American Library Association, 1997) describes how to make and use puppets in library storytimes and in other library programming. You don't have to be an expert seamstress or craftperson to make and use these puppets.

Another librarian, Rob Reid, has written a handy book called *Family Storytime: Twenty-Four Creative Programs for All Ages* (Chicago: American Library Association, 1999). Reid describes programs that will please all ages, from preschoolers to their older siblings to their parents, using books and songs to make storytime a celebration.

Would you like to memorize and perform a short story without holding a book in your hand? There are many great books for beginning storytellers. Look for the many books by Margaret Read MacDonald, including *Look Back and See: Twenty Lively Tales for Gentle Tellers* (New York: H.W. Wilson, 1991). These tales are brief enough to tell in just a couple of minutes and are easy to learn. In fact, MacDonald stresses that you don't have to memorize the stories word for word, but learn the stories so you can paraphrase and get your own rhythm. Another great handbook for the beginning storyteller is Nancy Schimmel's *Just Enough to Make a Story: A Sourcebook for Storytelling* (Berkeley, CA: Sisters' Choice, 1992). Some of her stories involve holding a prop, which allows for your nervous energy to be diverted.

For those who are too shy to even sing in the shower, check out *Little Hands Fingerplays and Action Songs: Seasonal Activities and Creative Play for 2- to 6-Year-Olds* by Emily Stetson and Vicky Congdon (Charlotte, VT: Williamson Publishing, 2001). You don't have to be able to carry a tune to sing a fingerplay, because the audience will soon drown you out!

Web Sites

Web sites offer many ideas for storytimes, and many of the suggestions are arranged by themes—holidays, animals, or food—listing books, songs, fingerplays, and crafts related to the theme. These Web sites can be a great help for those new to storytime, and they can help you cut down on the amount of preparation time needed.

A handy Web site, www.bayviews.org, lists storytime themes with craft ideas from the Association of Children's Librarians of Northern California. It includes a new theme each month in the storytime link.

Sponsored by the Utah Library Association, http://www.ula.org/organization/rt/csrt/csrt-storytm.htm offers storytime themes complete with suggestions for books, songs, fingerplays, and flannelboards. It also has craft ideas along with printable coloring sheets.

Perpetual Preschool (www.perpetualpreschool.com/) has lots of great storytime theme pages, each of which includes suggestions for books, games, songs, crafts, and simple science projects.

With over 300 storytime themes, www.thebestkidsbooksite.com/ storytimes.htm lists books, songs, and craft ideas for preschool storytimes that will help newcomers as well as longtime storytime readers.

One of the most useful Web sites for craft ideas is www.enchantedlearning.com. It has a wealth of printable activity sheets, as well as instructions for a wide variety of craft projects, most constructed with paper or other recyclable items. This site also has links to homework help.

Looking for songs or fingerplays for storytime? Try www.kididdles.com or www.songsforteaching.com/fingerplays/index.htm, both of which list lyrics to traditional preschool songs. You can even hear the melody of some of the songs.

STORYTIMES AT ANY LIBRARY

Storytime is one of the most rewarding aspects of children's services in a library. School librarians are finding that primary graders appreciate storytime as much as preschoolers, so they have incorporated storytime into the school library schedule. Storytime is a great way to outreach to new library users: Parents of very young children may not be literature readers themselves, but they know their children need books, and will soon appreciate the library's media and nonfiction books, like cookbooks, for themselves. Even if a small library is limited by funding, a storytime will be the one program that they hold due to its impact on the target audience and the modest preparation it entails. The staff will find it a highlight of the week, and it can be great for public relations opportunities like photos in the local newspaper or guest readers like the mayor for National Library Week. By starting out slowly with just one storytime per week, even novice children's staffers can quickly take to storytime and look forward to it!

Chapter 6

Programming

WHAT IS LIBRARY PROGRAMMING?

Public libraries conduct a wide variety of programs to encourage visits to the library and to promote great books to read. This chapter covers practical advice on hosting professional entertainment as well as conducting programs just with staff and volunteers, from magicians and puppet shows to organizing craft programs and hands-on science and history programs. A major focus is on library tours for teachers and their students. Book discussion groups for elementary and middle school children are presented, as well as tips on conducting summer reading programs with minimal staff. All the programming ideas are tied to books, since programs work as a promotional device to encourage reading.

Why Do Programming? The Library as Place

Having library programs promotes the library as a "town square," or central meeting place. The library becomes a valuable asset to the community, not just for books but as a cultural center. Good programming draws the community into the library and makes it easier to get the funds to stay open when budget cuts are proposed.

Non-English speaking families may not know the library has something for them, but if you hold a program celebrating their culture, they will discover the library has books in their languages, or tutoring. Especially when you feature programming for children, they will learn the library provides homework help for their children.

Librarians have been doing entertainment type programs since the 1970s to encourage use of the library and to promote reading. They hope to get families to visit the library in the summer especially and to get their children to join the summer reading program. Other programming will encourage more children to get library cards. Programming plans are made to highlight certain parts of the library collection and increase circulation of those items. The bottom line is to promote the library as a fun and cool place to go. Programming includes library tours and class visits, as well as instruction on how to find things in the library.

LIBRARY TOURS

Library tours for class visits are a fairly basic service but can be made more fun if approached in a creative way. Usually, the tours are scheduled by a teacher, who brings the students to the library, where you or a trained volunteer docent conducts the library tours. Expectations for school visits include "outreach" services: to get new library card holders.

Expectations for School Visits

A major expectation is to help students who do not have a library card to get one when they arrive. You will need a list of the students to see if they have a card, and if not, try to get teachers to turn in a class's applications at least two days before a tour so you can get new cards ready. Obviously, the younger the children the more likely they will need cards; older students usually have cards unless they have just moved to the community. Older students are more likely to owe fines or need replacement cards. See if you can get most of that settled before the tour if possible. Hopefully, students will all check out at least one book at the end of a library tour; therefore you will need to have new and replacement cards ready when students arrive or it will delay their departure.

You will need to find out the teacher's purpose for the visit. The teacher may have a goal in mind such as recreational reading books for Sustained Silent Reading time, or to remind children to come to the library over summer vacation (so the tour is scheduled in late May or early June). When the teacher wants the class to find books for their state reports or another topic they are expecting to research, I try to find a "hook," especially when covering the nonfiction area of the library. If you know the teacher has a big assignment coming up, if you show the books that relate to the assignment, the class will be more likely to focus.

Whatever the reason for the tour, this should be a welcoming event showing the students that they are welcome in the library and that the library has the resources they need for their classes. It is also a place where they can find fun books to read.

Scheduling Tours

Most teachers like morning best; even if your library doesn't open until 10:00 A.M., try starting tours at 9:00 A.M. One plus is that there are no other patrons to complain you are too loud. Doing tours before you open is best because you won't be interrupted during the tour. Usually the teacher phones and sets the tour and confirms it at that time. Teachers can be difficult to reach on the phone, so I don't usually do a follow-up call; but I make it clear when we talk that the visit is set. You can decide what works best for you. Perhaps you can confirm by e-mail a day or two before the tour is scheduled to make sure the class is still coming so you can have the materials you plan to show and the library cards ready for the visit.

Special Topics for Upcoming Assignments

You may want to pull books onto a cart for a special assignment if the teacher is bringing them to check out books for their state reports, the Civil War, or another topic. This is especially true if the assignment calls for books from different Dewey numbers. That Civil War report could include books from the Biography Section, 973.7 or a comparable Dewey number, or books on weapons or slavery from the 300 section.

Your Agenda versus the Teacher's

Try to get teachers to stay with the class, and the parents who come with the kids, too. Teachers and parents accompanying the class may need to be reminded, especially if the tour is scheduled before the library opens, that you are not open yet, so they don't wander off or interrupt other staff members who are still setting up to open on time.

Teachers may have unrealistic expectations for the visit. Many teachers have little concept of what is available in the library and how students can access information. They may want you to teach first graders how to use the public online catalog, but you can say that they are just too young. Your time is better spent showing them what the library contains and reading them a story. Or the teacher may want you to show the class how to do research; and that may not be possible during the short time they are at the public library. You should refer them back to the school librarian, or, if they don't have a school librarian, show the teacher any books that would be useful in the classroom on how to do research. It is okay to say "no" if the teacher asks you to cover something outside your area.

Making Tours Fun

If you give a lot of tours for young children, you can incorporate props. You can do several things to reach the visual, aural, and kinetic learners on a library tour.

Puzzles

Take a free book poster and glue it, using rubber cement, to some tagboard. Then cut it into a jigsaw puzzle of approximately eight pieces. Have a piece at each major area you are describing: the circulation desk, children's desk, picture books, magazines, videos/DVDs, easy readers, and encyclopedias, among others. The child who can answer a question based on what was just said gets to hold that puzzle piece: "Can you check out books for one, two, or three weeks?" or "Who wrote *Green Eggs and Ham*?" Then the children can put the puzzle together to see who is on the poster. This helps them pay attention to what you are saying. Puzzles can be especially useful for tours where children are under the age of eight.

Family Feud

Another game to help them focus is library "Family Feud." Have the group divide in half, then line up across from each other. One person from each team steps up to the buzzer: you can take one from a "Taboo" board game, or use a bell of some sort. Then ask a simple question such as, "If you lose your library card, how many dollars does it cost to get another card?" Children buzz in and try to answer; if the first child doesn't get it right, let the other team answer, just like on television's "Family Feud." It's fun and often ends in a tie or is very close. Give out bookmarks to everyone for playing. Let the winning team choose their bookmarks first. This game works best with children in grades two to five.

Trivia Game

Tours can be a time when, for children in third grade or older, you demonstrate how to use the library's catalog or how to access the Internet, depending on what the teacher had in mind for the tour. If the class is under third-grade age, not enough children in the class will be able to spell well enough to look things up. For a trivia game, find books that have activities on library use for students: crossword puzzles that reinforce what is covered on a library tour, Dewey Decimal games, authors and titles. You can also see if they can find trivia answers on the Internet. To make it even more fun, give out stickers and bookmarks as prizes.

Scavenger Hunt

A fun activity for an older class (fourth to sixth grades) is a scavenger hunt. Give everyone the same clues to make it fair, just put the clues in different order on the list so each team goes to a different area to start. A clue may be "Find a *Mad Magazine*," or "Find a book on taking care of a new puppy." This works especially well if the tour is held before the library opens so no one complains that you are making too much noise. The children will get really excited and run during a scavenger hunt, but it is worth the noise to see how much fun they are having in the library!

Remember, children are likely to remember only a few facts, so don't feel you were unsuccessful if kids can't remember too much. It also means you shouldn't go into too much detail, just give the highlights. But I know this really works; I have had children from a morning tour bring in a parent in the afternoon to get a card and show the parent the videos and DVDs, or something else remembered from the tour.

What to Cover

No matter what the teacher has in mind, there are things you will want to cover. You want to make clear the rules of check out, fines, and care of materials so no one is caught unaware. You also want to show all the fun stuff the library has. Be pleased if only one child goes home and talks about all the cool videos you have, or remembers you have comics or graphic novels. Some will come right after school to check out more materials even if they only took one book while their class was there. For the primary grades, read a fun story, usually library related: for kindergarten, try *I Took My Frog to the Library* by Eric Kimmel; for first grade, read *D.W.'s Library Card* by Marc Brown. Then go over what is the same and what is different about your library from the one in the story. Even second and third graders like to hear you read a story. For classes in fourth to eighth grades, it is nice if you have just a couple of minutes to do some very basic booktalks: "We have the new Lemony Snicket books, and check out our magazines for your grade: we have *MAD, Nickelodeon,* several video game magazines, *Teen People,* and *Popstar.*"

Tours can be a great way to introduce the library to new patrons, and those children will become regular library users if the tour is memorable and fun. But tours are just the "tip of the iceberg" when it comes to library programming; let's explore some other ways to motivate children to visit the library.

BOOK DISCUSSION GROUPS

Book discussion groups, whether they are called Readers Roundtable, Xtreme Readers, or something else, can be fun and very popular. They are not just for TV's *Oprah* anymore! The goal of a book discussion group is to encourage the love of recreational reading. It is not a remedial program; rather it is aimed at children who are comfortable with reading and want to be challenged.

These groups usually meet once a month to discuss a book that has been chosen for everyone to read. Because you may not be able to afford to buy additional copies of these books to give to each child, you may offer choices in obtaining the book to be read for that month's meeting. You could have students buy the paperback at cost, go to a bookstore to buy on their own, or have copies to check out if the library cannot give away the book for free. Perhaps the Friends of the Library can pay for extra copies for students unable to buy copies of the paperback.

Some librarians have noticed that boys may be hesitant to join or to stay with a book discussion group. I have been very lucky with our Xtreme Reader group, which is the book discussion group for fourth and fifth graders. From the beginning, we had as many boys as girls. I think part of the reason is the name: Xtreme Readers, like Xtreme Sports, sounds really cool and does not make you think of tea parties. The name was thought up by a boy who was a fourth grader at the time. His mother works at the library, and he was in the initial group. We put the name prominently on all our flyers, in a cool font and with a dramatic graphic of a person reading while skateboarding.

To kick off the club, we sent the flyers with a cover letter to all the GATE (gifted and talented) programs in the fourth and fifth grades (both public and private schools), because we felt our target audience would be children who already liked reading chapter books. We had a very good initial enrollment of boys and girls, fourth and fifth graders, in equal proportion. We also placed an article in the local paper. This and our library flyers helped to get the word out, especially to homeschoolers. Now children start the club at the beginning of summer vacation and the summer reading program because they have finished third grade and according to library policy, they are considered fourth graders during the summer before they actually begin fourth grade.

Activities Make It Fun

Besides the cool name Xtreme Readers, we always have lots of activities following the half-hour book discussion. Since a larger percentage of boys are kinetic learners, they need more hands-on activities. We all like hands-on activities, girls as well as boys, because these well-planned activities bring the books to life. Be thinking about hands-on activities as your read about the format for a book discussion club.

Format of Book Discussion Club

Everyone checks in at a place where they will pick up the book for next time. When they pick up their books for the next month, there is a question sheet included. These discussion questions are not homework but a jumpstart to help the kids focus on different parts of the book we plan to discuss, such as characters in the book. If you do groups for older students, like teens, you may not need to hand out discussion questions ahead of time.

Divide the attendees into circles of no more than fifteen children. You will need one adult to lead the twenty to thirty minutes of discussion for each circle. The adults can be reliable parent volunteers who have been trained to conduct the discussion, or other staff. The book discussion leaders do not have to be teachers or librarians. They can even be older high school students and college students if they have a great interest in reading and literature.

After the discussion has concluded, we move onto the hands-on activities, which are always related to the book, and finally a snack, which we try to relate to the story when possible. For example, after we discussed *Hatchet* by Gary Paulsen, the children had berries and water as their snack. Then they rotated around several different stations set up at separate tables. At one they had to identify different trees based on leaves we had collected. At another they did a simple first aid activity. At the third they did a word search puzzle.

All of the activities reinforced aspects of the plot or characters. Sometimes we do just one activity instead of having several stations. For *Bud Not Buddy* by Christopher Paul Curtis, everyone made posters about jazz music, similar to the one Buddy has in his suitcase, while we listened to jazz and Big Band music. We put the posters up at the library, too, and the children picked them up at the following meeting.

Periodically we will survey the children about books to use in future meetings. We don't take every suggestion, but the children often will give us great ideas or let us know not to use a book because everyone has already read it because it was assigned in school (such as *Number the Stars* by Lois Lowry). During these surveys, you can hear whether some think a book is too much of a "girl" book or too much of a "boy" book, although we hear more often if it is a "girl" book. Ann Martin's *The Doll People,* for example, was one the boys didn't seem interested in, just based on the title.

That doesn't mean you can't have books with girl protagonists. Many of our books do, and they were very popular with the boys in the club. These included *Because of Winn Dixie* by Kate DiCamillo, *Notes from a Liar and Her Dog* by Gennifer Choldenko, and *Mick Harte Was Here* by Barbara Park. Books that were less successful with the boys included *Out of the Dust* by Karen Hesse and *My Louisiana Sky* by Kimberly Willis Holt. I'm not sure why, but I don't think it was because there was a girl protagonist. Often you can find books with both a boy and a girl main character, such as *From the Mixed Up Files of Mrs. Basil E. Frankweiler* by E. L. Konigsburg, that appeal to everyone. You don't have to choose only books with boy protagonists. In fact, it wouldn't be fair if you did, and you underestimate boys if you do.

Resources for Book Discussion Group Ideas

If you haven't conducted a book discussion group before, several great resources will help you get started. When I was planning to start a group, I was inspired by *The Mother Daughter Book Club* by Shireen Dodson (New York: HarperCollins, 1997). Written by a parent who started a mother-daughter book club, it is filled with lots of common sense advice, sample questions, and outlines for discussion books that were used successfully.

Another invaluable resource is the Web site of the Mulnomah County, Oregon, library (http://www.multcolib.org/talk/index.html), which has suggestions for common discussion questions and outlines for book discussions of specific books. More than a hundred books are listed, along with questions tailored to that book and activity ideas!

Publishers' Web sites can also be very helpful in finding discussion questions for a book group. Scholastic Books' Web site (http://teacher.scholastic.com/products/tradebooks/discguide/) has an extensive listing of book discussion guides you can print out. Each book has a long list of discussion questions that will get even reluctant readers talking! HarperCollins is another publisher whose Web site (http://www.harperchildrens.com/teacher/) has great book discussion guides, with lots of discussion questions and interviews with the authors.

If you are just getting started, you may want to begin with a discussion group for fourth and fifth graders. Once that takes off, you can expand and begin a group for middle schoolers, then add a group of high school students. Meeting just once a month seems to work for all age groups, and book discussion groups could end up being one of your most satisfying job duties!

ENTERTAINMENT/MULTICULTURAL PROGRAMMING

Entertainment programs are very popular in public libraries. Librarians see that having a music concert, a magic show, an author talk, or a storyteller will draw an audience. Families will take the time in their busy schedules to visit the library if there is a special program being held. Entertainment programming can also bring in new users and "nonreaders." Nonreaders may come to see a concert and find out libraries offer a wealth of media to check out, not just books. These folks will become library users when a program draws them to visit the library.

Entertainment Programs

Should you hire professional entertainment or do it yourself? The ultimate way to judge this is to ask yourself, "Is this program worth the time/trouble of a busy parent, who has driven the child down to the library for this hour?" Also, will it draw enough attendance to be worth the library's time and money? A different standard is applied when it comes to attendance for teens than for younger children; teen programs generally draw smaller crowds. A family program with a professional entertainer should draw a large crowd (whatever your meeting room will hold). Also, you want only high-quality programs, that will add to your library's reputation. If your programs are consistently of a high quality you will build up a consistent audience.

To find great children's performers, network with other librarians in your area. Some groups may even hold auditions for persons interested in being placed on an "entertainers" list. Other children's librarians may list recommended performers related to the annual summer reading program theme on a Web site. If you are interested in hiring a performer who has not been recommended by another library, ask for an audition videotape or for references from other libraries or schools.

Even if you haven't seen the performer, you will want references from others who have seen the person perform for a family audience.

Working with Professional Performers

Professional performers want to make you happy; their continued employment often is based on word of mouth among librarians and teachers. To help them meet your expectations, communication is the key. You want to spell out your needs and limits ahead of time, and hear the performer's needs to help make the show a success. Some issues related to working with performers are discussed below.

Sales of CDs, Books, or Other Items

Clear this ahead of time. Some libraries have regulations that bar sales to patrons, but many do not. Public libraries often have the Friends of the Library organization sell the books or other items for a cut of the profits.

Payment

Be sure to cover payment beforehand with the performers. If your finance department does not allow you to pay on the day of the program, go over that with the performers so they know when to expect payment. Send any paperwork, for example, a W9 form, to the performers and let them know the date you need it to be returned.

Facility Constraints

Does the performer prefer to do the show inside or outside? If you must do the show outside, be sure to let the performer know that. Small libraries may find that outside is the only way to accommodate an audience, and some shows don't work outside. For example, a science show with bubbles is greatly affected by even a slight wind. Many magicians cannot have audience members behind them because it will reveal the secrets of the illusions.

When making plans for the show, be sure to include room for children with disabilities or special needs such as wheelchairs. Also, be sure to discuss the sound system needs with the performer. Some provide their own sound system, some do not, yet it can be the one element that impacts the success or failure of the program.

Publicity

You don't want to hold a program and have no one come! Publicity can be as simple and affordable as flyers sent to local schools; press releases in the local paper; and outreach to daycares, after-school programs, and Boys and Girls Clubs. If you have a sizable group of residents who don't speak English, get a staff member or volunteer to translate your flyer into the language to target new library users.

Planning

If you are holding the program outside, check the projected weather report. Make sure the gardener isn't planning to mow or water the lawn that day. Check that the date and time do not conflict with events at local schools or the recreation department. Make sure the other areas of the library do not have anything planned for that day such as a computer upgrade that affect the circulation department.

Tickets

If you need to predict and control the crowd at your program due to space limitations, you may want to give out free tickets to the show. When you have an overwhelming demand, you should try to schedule a second show that same day.

Hosting the Show

When performers have equipment they need to unload, reserving a parking space for them can be very helpful. They also need staff to act as ushers, controlling the crowd. They don't want to stop halfway through their shows to help a crying child in the front row who suddenly needs a parent! You need to treat the performer as you would wish to be treated if you were going to another library to do something. Good manners are all that is needed.

Multicultural Programs

Multicultural programs can a bring in new library users who before this felt the library only served English speakers or felt the library was "elitist." Do both special events, like "Black History Month" and "Cinco de Mayo," as well as multicultural events in the summer reading program. Female magicians, storytellers who include stories celebrating specific cultures, and dance groups from various cultures point out that you and your library recognize and celebrate diversity.

Multicultural programs can be very successful if you partner with community groups from those cultures. They can get the word out to their members who may have never been to the library before. They can put you in touch with performers or guest speakers on their cultures or set up an information booth on their organization. Ethnic restaurants may want to provide free refreshments to advertise their businesses. Having community partners for library events is always a plus, and with multicultural programming it can be especially helpful as a way to ensure the program reflects a culture accurately.

DO IT YOURSELF PROGRAMS

When a professional performer is too expensive or not relevant to the goal of library programming, many librarians conduct programs put on by the staff. You can celebrate certain books like Harry Potter or specific topics such as history, sports, science, or the arts. These either are aimed at a specific age group, such as middle schoolers, or may bring together many age groups for intergenerational programming. You and your library staff who conduct these "do-it-yourself" programs do not have to be experts. Many books and Web sites will give you ideas for doing a science program or an arts and crafts holiday program.

Arts

Librarians often conduct arts and crafts programs without hiring outside help. We already include crafts during some of our storytimes, and you can try a crafts program to celebrate the December holidays, Earth Day, or the start of spring. Arts and crafts programs can be part of your multicultural holiday celebrations, part of National Library Week or National Poetry Week (both of which are in April), or for National Children's Book Week in November. You can find many craft books and Web sites as a source for ideas. You will want to do a book display at the program, and the featured books will certainly circulate. If you need additional help during the program, you may call upon your volunteers or ask your high school patrons to volunteer.

History and Science

For programs celebrating history and science, set up four or five stations, each with a different hands-on activity. You will need two volunteers to help at each station. Begin the program by reading three or four picture books of interest to school age children, then break up the group, with children at each station. Remind them every five or ten minutes to rotate to a new station so they can do all the activities before it is time to go home.

For a program on American history, we read *Peppe the Lamplighter* by Elisa Bartone and then played marbles. Who knew such an old fashioned game would be so popular? For weeks afterward, children asked if they could borrow my marbles and play outside in the library patio. We also read Deborah Hopkinson's *Sweet Clara and the Freedom Quilt* and made quilt squares out of construction paper.

Our science program included a reading of Dan Yaccarino's *The Lima Bean Monster* followed by putting lima beans in wet paper towels and then placing them in plastic sandwich bags. We found the instructions on lima bean sprouting in several science experiment books. We also found recipes for Gak, which we made after reading *Bartholomew and the Oobleck* by Dr. Seuss. There are many science activities that will relate to picture books and will suit a program like this.

Storytelling Programs

Storytelling can appeal to a wider age range than preschool storytime. Try a do-it-yourself storytelling program, with arts and crafts. Many books are available to help you learn to perform stories, but a great introductory source is *Tell It Again! 2: Easy to Tell Stories with Activities for Young Children* by Rebecca Isbell and Shirley C. Raines (Beltsville, MD: Gryphon House, 2000). This very thorough handbook on storytelling for adults who work with preschoolers has a wealth of stories to tell, along with extension activities. While it is nice to have a professional storyteller when you can afford it, you can design entertaining programs by using this book and adapting your program for any older children who will attend.

Puppet Shows

Puppet shows can draw a very large audience to your library. It can be difficult as well as expensive to get a professional puppet show to visit if you are far away from a big city. Many librarians have learned to put on puppet shows themselves! If you would like to try puppetry, check out *A Show of Hands: Using Puppets with Young Children* by Ingrid M. Crepeau and M. Ann Richards (St. Paul, MN: Redleaf Press, 2003). This is a complete handbook on puppetry in the library and classroom, including how to make puppets and puppet scripts. One chapter goes into detail on using puppets with special needs students.

Another handy book is *How to Do "The Three Bears" with Two Hands: Performing with Puppets* by Walter Minkel (Chicago: ALA, 2000). Minkel is a librarian who has performed these puppet shows at his library. The book is a complete step-by-step guide on making and using puppets in the library, along with five puppet scripts. It also has advice on how to adapt books into scripts, and even directions on building a portable puppet theater.

Book-Themed Parties

Many librarians have conducted do-it-yourself programs celebrating popular fiction series, like Harry Potter, Captain Underpants, or Lemony Snicket. To hold a party on a favorite book series, check out the official Web site of that author and publisher. Many will have ideas for library activities that you can use for your party. Also, many Web sites put together by librarians will offer ideas for programs that were successful; these tried and true ideas have been tested so you know they could work for you. The listserv PUBYAC offers great programming ideas; it can be found at http://www.pubyac.org/. PUBYAC's Web site has an archive where you can find ideas that were posted previously. You may also want to join PUBYAC, since it is a great way to get advice on problems in your library or to find suggestions for patrons who remember the plot of a book but cannot remember the author or title.

AUTHOR/ILLUSTRATOR VISITS

Many libraries host visits by authors or illustrators. These can be a favorite library program, although they can be very expensive to hold. You can find many books and articles about hosting an author visit. Do some research to see what would work for you, but mostly, can you afford this?

An author needs to be paid for the time away from writing, and if the author is not local, you will also have to pay travel expenses. If you haven't held an author visit before, try starting out with a local author since that will be more affordable. Partner with a local bookstore manager, who may have contacts with publishers to help keep costs lower as well. If publishers are sending authors on a tour, they may be able to fit in a library program and not charge travel expenses since the author is already on the road.

If you host an author visit, you want a large audience to make it worth the cost. If you can partner with the local schools, they may help with funding and it will help increase the audience. You can even hold the program during the school day and have classes come to see the author as part of a field trip to the library. I have done this with great success, but you must plan this in advance, to make sure the classes can attend.

If you hold the program on a Saturday, publicize it to likely attendees. School book clubs, the Girl Scouts, tutoring programs, homeschoolers, and any other related group who may be interested should be notified. The Friends of the Library may want to sell the guest's books for a cut of the profits.

MOVIE PROGRAMS

Showing films can be a popular library program, drawing a wide age range of children. It is very important that you clear the rights to have a public showing of the film. A few videos and DVDs come with public performing rights, but most do not. One place to find out how to get a license to show a film to the public is to ask the Swank Motion Picture distributors at the Web site http://www.movlic.com/. They sell licenses to schools, libraries, recreation departments, and related groups for public film showings.

In the past, we used to show films on a 16 millimeter projector. Now many libraries show DVDs using a LCD projector. You also want to have a room and sound system that allow for viewing on a large screen. Try to get as close as possible to the real movie theater experience.

Usually you will get better attendance for a film showing if the movie has just come out on DVD. With so many great films adapted from children's novels, the first choice in film showings is a movie based on a children's book. Make a display of books by that author, or books with similar themes, so that attendees can find books to take home with them.

REFRESHMENTS

Many libraries do not allow food in the building, but an exception should be made for refreshments at library programs. Food just seems to inspire more people to attend the program or to stay until the end because that is the best time to serve the food. Food also makes the program seem more like a celebration! Even a lecture can end on a "fun" note with cake or ice cream. Ethnic foods are a great way to conclude a multicultural program. You can also find healthy snacks if you are concerned about setting a good example. Fruit or sorbet can satisfy a sweet tooth as well as candy. Since many children are allergic to nuts and peanuts, I try to avoid those. Sometimes local bakeries or restaurants will donate refreshments for a library program.

SUMMER READING PROGRAMS

Many librarians in public libraries envy those who work in schools, because the summer can be exhausting due to the popularity of summer reading programs. On the other hand, the summer reading program can be very satisfying, because it can create lifelong readers and library users. Many school librarians are adapting summer reading program themes, incentives, and games to motivate recreational reading at school, especially during winter and spring breaks.

How Summer Reading Programs Work

The summer reading program is basically a drop-in program where children get a reading log or journal; keep track of books, pages, or time spent reading; and bring the journal back to show the library to get prizes and other incentives. A few librarians have the children write a short, one-paragraph book review, and younger children draw a picture about the book. Most libraries have children record the title only. More and more, librarians find it more equitable for kids to record minutes or pages read. Many librarians require between eight and ten books, or the equivalent pages or time spent reading, to complete the summer reading program. Some even let the child and parent set the goal. The main reasons for holding a summer reading program include motivating children to come to the library during the summer, increasing circulation, enabling children to maintain their reading skills between one grade and the next, and developing positive attitudes toward the library and reading. So don't be the "reading police." Many children read below grade level, so reading a short book may be all they can handle; yet they have worked as hard as their friends who read above level. Also, the summer reading program isn't just for children who are independent readers but includes children who are read to by parents and caregivers.

Rewards and Incentives

Arguments continue over giving out prizes for reading. Some librarians say "Reading is its own reward," and some educators have conducted studies that say incentives do not work; however, many librarians know that incentives get borderline readers to read during summer vacation. Many children would read anyway, but some, and more boys than girls, won't make time for recreational reading without the incentives offered by the summer reading program. Do a little research on the Internet and you will find opinions across the board. A more relevant survey could be done with librarians in your area to see what they do and what has worked for them in the past. They could be the best model for what you may want to try.

If you decide that you need incentives, local museums and amusement parks can be a great resource for no-cost incentives. They may give the library free passes to distribute, knowing the child will need to be accompanied by a parent who pays for admission. In this way they create new customers for the museum or business.

Games

Most summer reading programs have a game board or other game element to make it fun and to help record reading progress. A typical game is to spin a wheel after the child has read one book; the spinner may decide what incentive is earned. Or readers will get a game board and move along the spaces based on how many pages they have read; when they land on specific squares on the game board they may choose a prize. Be sure the game is based on chance, not skill. Make it fair to all ages and abilities, such as a game similar to spinning a wheel, picking a game piece out of a hat, and other games of chance. The summer reading game, game boards, and other elements can vary depending on the library. A great book for those starting a summer reading program for the first time is *Fiore's Summer Library Reading Program Handbook* by Carole D. Fiore (New York: Neal Schuman, 2005). Written by a children's librarian, the book covers every detail of designing and running a summer reading program.

Themes

Most librarians pick a theme for their summer reading program. Then they want "accessories" to go along with it, such as reading logs, posters, bookmarks, and stickers. These are often available from library merchandise companies. Demco and Highsmith offer themed program items that will work with children. These have a cost associated with their selection, so you may need help from Friends of the Library or other groups to sponsor the purchase of these items.

Many states also will sponsor an annual summer reading program with a new theme each year. Find out what your state offers. If they do, this could save you a lot of money since they offer items at a low price based on the purchasing power of the whole state. More than forty states participate in the Collaborative Summer Library Program; check the Web site (http://www.cslpreads.org/index.html). This is a consortium of states that work together to choose the annual theme for a children's and a teen summer reading program. See if your state is a member and what the CSLP has to offer in the way of graphics, posters, and other materials.

PROGRAM EVALUATION

Evaluating whether a program has been successful shouldn't be a major research study. It is usually simple mathematics. How many people attended? If the meeting area was three-quarters full, consider it a great success. Did the program attract any new users or new library card holders? If the answer is, "yes," that is always a plus. Did parents feel it was worth their time, so they will want to attend a library program in the future? If you consistently have quality programs, you will eventually have a built-in audience who will return to your programs based on your past success.

Publicizing Your Successes

Don't just publicize your programs in advance. Send a photo and press release of a program that has just finished to your local paper. It is good publicity for the library in general and creates buzz that the library has great programs. People will look for notices of future programs if they see articles on past programs.

You will want to tell your Friends of the Libraries about your successful programming if they have helped to fund any part of it. Your director and library board members also need to know. They can use examples of successful programs when budget time comes.

PROGRAMS: BOOKS ARE THE BASIS

Whether it is a book discussion group, a magic show, a Black History Month festival, or a summer reading program activity, books should be the basis of library programming. Books can help us in planning a do-it-yourself science program. They can even inspire a film showing since so many great movies are based on children's books.

Do a special display of books and media items related to the program, and you will encourage reading and increase circulation. If those who attend your magic show are not aware of it, show them the books and videos on how to be a magician. New library visitors who bring their children for a storytime may not know the library circulates CDs but will see the display. Programs first and foremost are a method of getting potential patrons into the library, both library users and people who haven't been to the library before.

Programs are a way to promote areas of the library collection to increase circulation of those items. Programs also show that the library is a cultural center, a vital meeting place for the community. So you must plan and conduct library programs. They will add excitement and may convince new users that the library has something for them.

Chapter 7

Issues in Children's Library Service

CHALLENGES IN SERVING CHILDREN IN LIBRARIES

Libraries of all sizes are facing challenges in service to children based on the changing dynamics of families, communities, and funding for children's services. Most of these relate to access issues and barriers to access. Families now may be led by a single parent or have both parents working, and their children need access to a safe place until their caregivers get home. Some parents are unaware of the services of the public library. Other parents have children with disabilities who must have access to the library. In some homes the income does not allow for access to the Internet. Many communities do not fund their schools well enough to provide for credentialed school librarians in their school libraries, and children lack access to school-related materials for their research. Finally, children's librarians must be aware of all aspects of the budget process so they can ensure that the children's program is adequately funded within the total library budget, or the materials and services to which children have access will be seriously limited. Finally, children's librarians need to be prepared to meet censorship challenges.

To help meet these challenges, this chapter discusses the meaning of access, assisting latchkey youth, providing children's access to the Internet and materials, and providing outreach to those who are unaware of the library or who have difficulty visiting the library. Tips on ensuring that children with physical disabilities as well as autism and developmental or learning disabilities are welcomed in library programs are provided. Suggestions are made for assisting teachers in schools where there is no school library or librarian. Overcoming censorship issues is a major challenge. Suggestions are made to help solve some problems before you take them to your library director.

WHAT IS ACCESS?

When librarians speak of "access" as an issue, we are talking about the ability of our patrons to find the information or resources they desire. Access can be as basic as a library being open on evenings and weekends when more people can use it, or as complicated as the ability of children to access information that may only be available on the Internet.

Librarians also talk about barriers to access. Sometimes official rules and policies can be a barrier to access. For example, prohibiting children from using a computer to type their reports limits access. Some libraries set aside computers just for students to use for homework so that this essential service is available. Cultural barriers exist if librarians cannot speak another's language or do not understand their patrons' backgrounds. Libraries can use bilingual volunteers to help eliminate this barrier. Many immigrants come from countries where the library is not a free service. They may be reluctant to come to the library, thinking that whatever they do or use there will have a fee attached. Outreach to new immigrant groups in your community can be a way to reduce cultural barriers to library service.

Other barriers exist in the way librarians treat their clientele. When a staff member is unfriendly to a child with autism because of the noises the child makes, that is a barrier to access. Many barriers to access can be reduced or eliminated just by better customer service. Do we treat all our patrons (including children) with kindness and patience? Is the library open when it is most beneficial to our residents, even if that means staff will need to work evenings and weekends? Do we look for new funding like grants to make sure we have the materials our patrons want? Let's look at some of the key concerns regarding library access for children.

LATCHKEY CHILDREN

Whether you live in a small or large community, access to a safe place after school for children who have no caregiver at home is a challenge. A variety of challenges exist when you have to serve latchkey children in the library. This is a national issue. Sure, we want young people using our libraries after school. The problem starts when a student is forced to wait at the library, with nothing to do, for hours until a parent picks up that child. Children who get bored can misbehave. When students have completed homework, used the allotted computer time, and are now just hanging out, their behavior can be disruptive to others and will act as a barrier to their use of the library. They block the front of the library, noisily talking, playing, and littering, or they take up tables and chairs needed by others. This is a concern each librarian needs to resolve at some point.

First, you can set limits. A common rule is that a person sitting at a library table should be using library materials. This may be necessary to free up space from people just hanging out in the library, no matter what their ages. Another common aspect is to enforce existing rules, such as no eating in the library and speaking quietly. Some librarians will designate meeting room space as a homework center for students who just need a space to sit and work on homework while waiting for a parent to pick them up, but who do not need library materials for that homework.

At What Age Can a Child Be Left Alone?

Another issue regarding latchkey children can be the age of the children. Most libraries have a set age limit. For some, a child must be at least age eight to be in the library without adult supervision. Some larger cities have had to set this age limit higher; students need to be at least in middle school to be on their own. These rules are not because a child is doing something wrong; they are for the safety of the child. You, with the approval of the library administration, must create and enforce rules for library use by latchkey children. Library administrators may need to check with the city attorney or law enforcement to determine the legal age limit for these children.

If children under that age limit are left unattended, the first step is to have the children phone the parent or caregiver to be picked up. If that is not possible, the librarian may need to speak to the parents when they do come and pick up the child, and then inform the parents of the rule. The librarian should not give the same parent repeated warnings. Once it is determined that a parent was spoken to before, call law enforcement. This is for the child's safety. It is true for young children left unattended or children left after closing time. If you are sure the parent knows the rule and is just disregarding it, be sure to call family services or law enforcement so they can see if there is a pattern of child abandonment. That may seem harsh, but with the epidemic of kidnapped children, helping to keep official records on unattended children may be the only way to prevent a missing child.

Often the biggest latchkey problems are older children, ages ten to thirteen, who are old enough to be in the library unattended but who misbehave due to boredom. You should be confident in sending misbehaving patrons, no matter what their ages are, out of the library. It is helpful to have a written policy stating the library rules so that they don't seem arbitrary. If the rule is no food in the library, you can point to that when asking someone to leave if they won't listen to your first request to take the food outside. If you don't have a written rule, the person may think you are sending him or her out just because you don't like his or her age, or race, or other personal factor. For more on dealing with latchkey children, check out *Unattended Children in the Public Library: A Resource Guide* (Chicago: American Library Association, 2002).

Homework Centers as a Solution

Some librarians have found the best solution in setting up a homework center for latchkey kids, so they have a separate room where they can eat, talk, or play games as well as do their homework. Many children do not have a parent who can help them with homework because of language barriers or other concerns, so a homework center can offer a safety net for some kids. It can also make the library more customer friendly to adults who would avoid the library if it was full of misbehaving kids, or more accessible to a student needing the library for research, but who cannot find an empty seat.

If you decide on setting up a homework center, books and Web sites are available to give examples of how to start. Many grants or other alternative funding sources are available for after-school programs and for homework centers. Also, most high school students are now required to do volunteer service for certain classes and for college admission needs, so they could be a resource of free tutors. Rather than constantly chasing noisy kids out of the library, many librarians have found a homework center room a great solution that is a positive, not a negative, activity that makes the library a more pleasant place as well as meeting a community need.

BEHAVIOR PROBLEMS

No matter what the person's age, misbehaving patrons should be dealt with because they are a barrier to access for others. A noisy child will push others who need a quiet place out of the library. Any person who takes up a computer beyond the established time limit prevents others' access to that computer. So long as everyone is treated fairly, asking students to stop unacceptable behavior is not a barrier to access; enforcing the rules actually opens up access for everyone else. To a child, the idea of fairness is very important. Children appreciate limits and will follow rules, especially if you are clear about what the rules are.

Many public libraries partner with the school district to enforce rules. If kids are hanging out at the library in the morning of a school day, ask why they are there instead of at school. Many school districts have a rule that children who are sick or on suspension must be in the care of a parent or caregiver, they are not permitted to hang out at the mall or the library. You should check with school district officials to learn the rules for children who are not at school during the school day. The library is not a suitable place for sick children or for students who are hanging out while cutting school.

ACCESS TO COMPUTERS AND THE INTERNET

More and more, students are required to turn in assignments in a typed form, even children as young as fourth grade. Since many families do not have a home computer, the library may be the only place where a student can use a computer to type homework and reports. Also, teachers now require that some research projects use the Internet, and many children do not have Internet access at home, so again the library is the only place where they can complete this part of their homework. Access to computers and the Internet in a library can be the difference between passing and failing for some students.

Many libraries require a parent to sign a consent form, often when the child is obtaining a library card, which permits him or her to use the Internet. What can you do if a student does not have a parent's permission to use the Internet? When a parent does not want their children to use the Internet, but a teacher requires it, the library may need to look for the Web site and print out the information using a staff computer. If the research is very brief, for example, the answer to a question, "Who is my congress person?" the librarian prints out the information for the student. If the homework requires more research, the library can inform the parent that a homework assignment requires Internet use to complete. Once parents know that, the parent can sit with the child at the computer, or give permission to use the Internet, or talk to the teacher. The librarian has taken care of the situation by informing the parent when the Internet may be a necessity. Following that, it is always up to the parent to decide whether or not a child can have computer or Internet access.

PROVIDING OUTREACH

One barrier to access to library services is the fact that some of our residents are unaware of what a library does. If they are new to the United States, they may come from a place where children are not welcome at libraries, where libraries do not circulate material, or where such services have fees attached to their use. Some countries run their libraries as research-only facilities, intended for university students. So you may need to do outreach to new U.S. residents, letting them know what your library offers for youth. You can make sure local agencies, clubs, churches, and other facilities that serve these new residents have your library flyers to let them know what is available.

Non-English Speakers

More communities are seeing non-English speakers in their schools, so we know that their families may not speak English in the home. Librarians can partner with schools to find out what other languages are spoken by students, and prepare flyers in those languages. Maybe there are local non-English newspapers that will help you promote library services to their readers. If you can publicize your library's services to non-English speakers, they will understand that they should bring their children to the library to use your services and your collections. They will flock to your library to find media, books, computers, and other resources once they know these items are available for them and their children as free services.

Literacy Programs

Many public libraries now have literacy programs for adults who want to improve their reading skills. One out of five adults who speaks English cannot read at a sixth-grade level, which means they cannot read the newspaper. While this may not seem directly applicable to children's programming, it has a direct relationship. Literacy programs can bring in new library users, because their increased literacy skills will make them comfortable enough to try cookbooks, home improvement books, and other informational books even if they do not become literature readers. They will model for their children the need for library resources in their lives.

In a more direct application, literacy programs often have a Families for Literacy component, which is a service to the families of their adult learners. You should partner with the Families for Literacy program, because it gives children's books to the families, and even does monthly storytimes. You can help by assisting the Project Literacy person, who may not have any experience with children's books, in choosing the books to be given out to those who attend. Children's staff can also help by offering to conduct the Families for Literacy storytimes, especially if a staff member already does a regular preschool storytime. You can repeat the same stories, songs, and crafts.

Some Project Literacy programs partner with local Head Starts, by sending trained volunteers to read to the children and give out free books. Children's staff can help in training the volunteers in choosing great read-aloud picture books and learning songs. You can even offer book bags with the read-alouds already collected, along with a puppet or other prop the volunteer can use at the Head Start visit.

INCLUSION OF CHILDREN WITH DISABILITIES AND NON-ENGLISH SPEAKERS

Librarians are attempting to provide more materials and services for children with special needs. Librarians are finding that a large number of users can benefit from books on tape and CD, including students with vision impairment or blindness, students with learning disabilities such as dyslexia, students learning English, and kinetic learners. The Internet or online sources are available in a wide range of languages; this can be a great benefit when a library serves students who don't read English very well, and when books in other languages are not available. Most DVDs have closed captioning, which can help those with hearing disabilities, or subtitles in other languages.

Some disabilities may cause children to speak too loudly or make noise; autism can cause children to yell out inadvertently. Try to be tolerant of these differences; it is not as if the child can control the behavior. Unless the behavior makes it very difficult for others to use the library, try to compromise; if it is just mildly annoying then let it go. Sign language can be effective with both autistic as well as deaf children; see if a volunteer can sign at your storytime or other programs, and you may have more children attend because this added service makes the library more accessible to them. Whenever possible, try to make a storytime or program available to all children, instead of offering a storytime just for kids with disabilities; the current trend is for inclusion. Both children with special needs and children without disabilities benefit from being together in storytimes, programs, or other educational situations since this allows for more socialization and teaches tolerance of others. Advertise that your summer reading program is for children with "all abilities," which implies those with disabilities are welcome, too.

To include more non-English speakers, see if there is staff development money available for training for those who are willing to learn another language. Also, try to encourage bilingual people to apply for jobs at the library, or to be library volunteers. Having a volunteer who can translate can be a huge asset, and it helps to show the community that the library values all its residents, including non-English speakers. Try having a bilingual storytime, or bilingual after-school tutors, if your community has a sizable group of students who are still learning English.

WEB SITES

Linda Lucas Walling is a professor of Library and Information Science at the University of South Carolina, and author of *The Disabled Child in the Library: Moving into the Mainstream,* co-written by Marilyn H. Harrenbrock (1985). Walling's Web site (http://www.libsci.sc.edu/facst/walling/bestfolder.htm) offers guidelines for evaluating children's books that depict disabilities, and lists of recommended children's books that show the disabled.

Part of the National Center for Education Statistics, the Web site http://nces.ed.gov/surveys/frss/publications/95357/ is a report on "Services and Resources for Children and Young Adults in Public Libraries." It gives statistics on what services are available to youth using public libraries, as well as barriers to services. It will give you an idea of what is statistically the norm, so you can gauge where your library fits in the scheme of things.

Provided by the Association of Library Service to Children, a division of the American Library Association, the Web site http://www.ala.org/ala/alsc/alscresources/forlibrarians/Chldrnnwithdisabilities.htm is a list of books and articles on serving special needs children in the library.

INCLUSION IS KEY

When dealing with latchkey children, children with special needs, or families still learning English, inclusion is the key. See if you can find a solution that allows people to find what they need; sometimes that just means finding a Web site in their language, or making sure library programs have space for wheelchairs. Inclusion also means enforcing behavior rules, so no one feels bullied at the library. That could mean asking loud kids to wait outside for parents, so that others can concentrate while in the library. That also means allowing a little more noise in the children's room and reserving seats in that area for children; adults who are not with children should not take up seats in the children's room.

Some areas of access to the library are up to the parent; only parents can give permission for their children to have library cards or to use the Internet. But parents cannot leave small children unattended, expecting the library staff to act as babysitters, and parents cannot leave children at the library after closing time due to safety concerns. So long as the rules and policies are clear and enforced equitably, fair access will occur. After all, why have a great book collection or wonderful programs if people are not comfortable coming to the library, or if the library is open for such limited hours that it does not meet the needs of the community? The library staff should monitor these needs and make the library as comfortable and accessible as possible, to people of all ages, so that we create lifelong library users.

ASSISTING TEACHERS

Since elementary schools in many locations do not have a librarian, teachers will visit the public library to find books to supplement the textbooks they use. If a teacher drops in after school and wants help in finding books for a unit on a particular subject, Pioneer Days for example, it may be difficult to help the teacher while managing the many children in the library. Try to encourage teachers to phone ahead if they need curriculum support. A teacher who just needs a certain book is an easier task. That can be easy to find on a drop-in basis, but if a teacher needs twenty nonfiction books on pioneers, and twenty historical fiction books featuring pioneers, encouraging them to phone ahead actually will save time. Once teachers realize it saves them time, they will be glad to call in requests.

Having this kind of arrangement with teachers will cause you much less frustration and will provide you the time needed to do a thorough search. Try pulling books requested by teachers in the morning before it is busy, so a teacher can pick them up later in the afternoon. Otherwise, if teachers drop in after school, you can start them at the online catalog, but you may not be able to do much more than that if the library is packed with children and others needing your attention.

Another service you can offer teachers is a "teachers' shelf" of teacher resource books that are available at teacher stores. Often a teacher will just need one craft idea or other short excerpt from one of these books, and it would be expensive for a teacher to purchase these. If the public library carries these, you will get many teachers visiting you who will be happy to photocopy the one thing they need out of a more expensive book, and they may check out more books. Many of these teacher resource books will also have craft and activity ideas the librarian can use at preschool storytime or at a book discussion group meeting, so they can be a great asset to a library.

If the school has a librarian, teachers will still need materials from the public library, but the school librarian can be one of your best allies. The school librarian can help distribute information to teachers, make arrangements for classes who want field trips to the library, or keep you informed about special projects or homework needs so you can prepare ahead of time. Try to make contact with the school librarian at the beginning of every school year so he or she knows your name, phone number, and e-mail address.

If you would like to visit schools, contact either the school librarian or the administration to make those arrangements. Remember, class time is very valuable, so make sure your presentations will be exciting, professional, well planned, and effective. With the No Child Left Behind testing, classes have very little "extra" time, so make the little time you are given the best it can be. You might want to visit the schools in late May or early June to promote the summer reading program, so you want your presentation to be brief but effective in getting out your message. Teachers want their students to read over summer vacation and will want to endorse your program if it seems worthwhile.

RESOURCES ON CENSORSHIP

One event that no library staff member looks forward to is the irate parent who complains that a book in the library is inappropriate for children; we all need to prepare ahead of time for such a complaint, whether it is a book on a controversial topic such as evolution, a book the parent feels is racist or sexist, or one that contains an obscenity. It may not be just books, but music CDs and videos and DVDs, that inspires a challenge.

Librarians need to prepare ahead of time for such an incident by having a selection policy and a formal procedure for patrons who wish to ask for an item to be removed. This policy comes through your governing body. If you have no policy, check procedures at other libraries and develop a policy before you actually receive a challenge. Decide who should take the complaint. Have a form for staff to give the patron. Sooner or later we all will receive such a challenge, so be prepared.

A great book that libraries will find useful when dealing with the issue of censorship is *Intellectual Freedom for Children: The Censor Is Coming* (Chicago: American Library Association, 2000). This should be read by library directors to help form policy, and by librarians and other staff who carry out the library's policies on challenges to library materials. Many libraries have a form for parents to fill out if they believe the library has a children's book that is inappropriate. Even very popular books, like the Harry Potter series, have been challenged by parents. Be sure to check with your administrators to see if policies and procedures are in place for dealing with challenges to library materials by parents. The American Library Association has an Intellectual Freedom "first aid kit" that contains sample forms and policies that work when dealing with censorship and challenges. To find out more, go to http://www.ala.org/ala/oif/intellectual.htm.

Often parents just want the complaint to be heard; they may not even want to fill out the form or have the book removed. They just want to be listened to; common courtesy and great customer service skills will always make receiving a challenge go smoother. Try to be objective and neutral; take the comments and let the patron know you will pass the challenge along to the supervisor. In some cases, the parents may be correct and the novel they are concerned about may be better suited to the Young Adult shelves. Often complaints reflect a very small segment of the population, and the book will be on assigned reading lists or have other reasons for staying in the library; offer the concerned parents alternatives that may be more in line with what they want for their children. Often this will satisfy the parents and they won't want to take the complaint any further. One reason we do weeding is to help us avoid such complaints; if we weed archaic materials that use language we would now consider racist or sexist, we will avoid some of these complaints. We cannot weed all of these of course, since some classics on the schools' assigned reading lists will use language that not everyone will be comfortable with.

INCREASING SERVICE THROUGH THE USE OF VOLUNTEERS

Volunteers can make a big difference in a library: they can assist at storytimes and programs, they can monitor the library computers, they can shelve certain items, and they can even tutor if given the proper training. Often high school students must volunteer for school credit (often this is called community service), retired people find volunteer work very satisfying, and adults want to give back to their community so they will try to find time to volunteer. Have you considered using volunteers at your library?

Recruiting Volunteers

Check if your library, city, or school district has a volunteer coordinator to help you recruit volunteers. Often all you will need is a brief article in the local paper, or a flyer to high schools and senior centers that will bring in volunteers. You should check on what procedures are called for at your library; it is common for adult volunteers who work with youth to be fingerprinted before they can begin volunteering. Many retired teachers find the library a great place for volunteering and they are a natural fit to be tutors or storytime assistants.

Activities to Assign to Volunteers

Every library has to determine what is best for volunteers to do, but often they can work in the children's department. Interview each volunteer as you would a job applicant to see where he or she will fit best in the library. If someone doesn't enjoy customer service but likes arranging things in order, shelving media or fiction could be a good job for that person and free up the paid shelvers to organize the more complicated Dewey sections or to shelf read. If volunteers are retired teachers who miss working with students, they might really enjoy tutoring children in the homework center after school, or may enjoy assisting at storytimes. Some also make very good docents, giving library tours or leading class visits, or assisting at other programs. Computer fans can be computer docents who monitor whose turn it is to use the computers in the children's room, or help those doing word processing or other programs, freeing up the librarian to help students find books.

Some volunteers, especially teens, are bilingual and can assist with translation, help at bilingual storytimes, or help students who are still learning English in the homework center. Some duties are better left to staff, like handling money or making library cards, since confidentiality and privacy issues are involved, although there may be exceptions. Readers' advisory and more complex teaching tasks, like giving orientation on using online resources or assisting teachers, are probably better left to staff. But there is more than busywork for volunteers to do; their assistance can be a big difference in the customer service we can give.

Training Volunteers

Training volunteers can be as important as training a new staff member, especially if you think the volunteer will be around for a long time. Volunteers should receive a library tour and orientation on the library's policies and basic procedures (such as how to answer the phone at a public service desk). High school volunteers who only need to do a few hours of community service may not need in-depth training but should still receive a library tour and some basic rules on customer service.

One time of year when you may be inundated with teen volunteers is summer vacation. I find the help given by teen volunteers well worth the time it takes to train and supervise them. Many high school age students are expected to do community service. Even if this is not a program in your schools, teens can assist with the registration, monitoring, prize distribution, and other elements of the summer reading program, freeing the librarian to do readers' advisory. Teen volunteers can also shelve books, since summer reading programs can greatly increase circulation.

If you haven't had success with teen volunteers, maybe they were too young. Sometimes middle school children are more difficult to train and manage than high school students. Although you may need to set an age limit, they can be great volunteers. For example, if the volunteers are bilingual, they make new library users feel more welcome and can help with programming and tutoring.

If you need a large group of volunteers for a special event such as a book sale, contact the local high schools; many have service clubs including Key Club, Octagon, Interact, and others that will send high school volunteers who will help set up and clean up as well as help customers. Teen service clubs can assist at larger library programs, such as the celebration that concludes the summer reading program, or special cultural events like Lunar New Year or Black History Month. Many of the teens may remember when they were preschoolers in your storytime and will enjoy helping at the library!

FUNDING

Do you know what percentage of your library's circulation is children's material? You may be surprised; children's books often are a bigger percentage of circulation compared to adult books, and media may even be bigger than either children's or adult books. Find out what areas of the collection circulate the most, and what areas of children's are the most popular. You may be spending most of your money on children's nonfiction, when fiction may be more popular. Some budget decisions should reflect these statistics, so you have the materials that your patrons want.

When it comes time for the yearly budget, be prepared with statistics for the administration, even before they ask! If everyone knows that young people make up more than half your visitors, which is very common in small libraries as well as large, that could ensure that the children's department gets a fair piece of the budget. If times are tough, all areas may have to take cuts, but they should be proportionate to circulation figures and statistics on library visitors and use.

These same figures will be very helpful in writing applications for grants that can compensate for some of the budget cuts most libraries are experiencing. Some grants are available without a lot of paperwork, and many small grants can add up! Check out what may be available in your area.

CONCLUSION

The issues and concerns of library service to children are an ever-changing topic; twenty years ago we didn't think about children's access to the Internet or computers, and forty years ago many libraries didn't think about latchkey children. In the future, we may have more concerns regarding technology, especially if the library is the only place where the working class may have access to computers and certain materials that will only be online. We may be more concerned that libraries are closing on nights and weekends due to budget cuts, yet more of our patrons need to come during those hours due to work schedules. We may find fewer preschoolers able to attend a library storytime, since many more are in daycare and cannot get to the library, so we may need creative solutions for how to bring reading to them.

But some things won't change; our patrons still need good customer service. The children's staff will need to advocate for funding for children's materials and services. More of our residents will need assistance in other languages besides English, and their children may need more homework help since there may not be anyone in the home who can speak English. The percentage of children with special needs, especially autism, is growing, and libraries need to find ways to reach out to those children and to serve them while still serving our other patrons. Creative solutions to many of these challenges are tried at libraries every day; professional journals, Web sites, and listservs help us network with each other to publicize those solutions that work. The children we serve certainly deserve the best we can give them!

Bibliography: Suggested Readings

Barr, Catherine, and John T. Gillespie. *Best Books for Children: Preschool through Grade 6.* 8th ed. Westport, CT: Libraries Unlimited, 2005.

Bauer, Caroline Feller. *New Handbook for Storytellers.* Chicago: American Library Association, 1995.

Bromann, Jennifer. *Booktalking That Works.* New York: Neal-Schuman Publishers, 2001.

Champlin, Connie. *Storytelling with Puppets.* 2d ed. Chicago: American Library Association, 1997.

Cobb, Jane. *I'm a Little Teapot!* Vancouver: BC: Black Sheep Press, 2001.

Connor, Jane Gardner. *Children's Library Services Handbook.* Phoenix, AZ: Oryx Press, 1990.

Crepeau, Ingrid M., and M. Ann Richards. *A Show of Hands: Using Puppets with Young Children.* St. Paul, MN: Redleaf Press, 2003.

Day, Frances Ann. *Latina and Latino Voices in Literature for Children and Teenagers.* Portsmouth, NH: Heinemann, 1997.

Dodson, Shireen. *The Mother Daughter Book Club.* New York: HarperCollins, 1997.

Dresang, Eliza. *Radical Change: Books for Youth in a Digital Age.* New York: H.W. Wilson, 1999.

Ernst, Linda L. *Lapsit Services for the Very Young: A How-to-Do-It Manual.* New York: Neal-Schuman, 1995.

Fiore, Carole D. *Fiore's Summer Library Reading Program Handbook.* New York: Neal Schuman, 2005.

Gillespie, John T. *The Children's and Young Adult Literature Handbook: A Research and Reference Guide.* Westport, CT: Libraries Unlimited, 2005.

Glazer, Joan I., and Cyndi Giorgis. *Literature for Young Children.* 5th ed. Upper Saddle River, NJ: Prentice Hall, 2004.

Greene, Ellin. *Books, Babies, and Libraries: Serving Infants, Toddlers, and Their Parents and Caregivers.* Chicago: American Library Association, 1991.

Isbell, Rebecca, and Shirley C. Raines. *Tell It Again! 2: Easy to Tell Stories with Activities for Young Children.* Beltsville, MD: Gryphon House, 2000.

Jeffery, Debby Ann. *Literate Beginnings: Programs for Babies and Toddlers.* Chicago: American Library Association, 1995.

Lewis, Valerie V., and Walter M. Mayes. *Valerie and Walter's Best Books for Children: A Lively, Opinionated Guide—Revised and Updated.* New York: HarperCollins, 2004.

Lima, Carolyn W., and John A. Lima. *A to Zoo: Subject Access to Children's Picture Books.* 7th ed. Westport, CT: Libraries Unlimited, 2005.

MacDonald, Margaret Read. *Look Back and See: Twenty Lively Tales for Gentle Tellers.* New York: H.W. Wilson, 1991.

Minkel, Walter. *How to Do "The Three Bears" with Two Hands: Performing with Puppets.* Chicago: American Library Association, 2000.

Minkel, Walter, and Roxanne Hsu Feldman. *Delivering Web Reference Services to Young People.* Chicago: American Library Association, 1999.

Nichols, Judy. *Storytimes for Two-Year-Olds.* 2d ed. Chicago: American Library Association, 1998.

Odean, Kathleen. *Great Books for Boys.* New York: Ballantine Books, 1998.

Odean, Kathleen. *Great Books for Girls.* New York: Ballantine Books, 2002.

Price, Anne. and Juliette Yaakov. *Children's Catalog: Eighteenth Edition.* New York: H.W. Wilson, 2001.

Rand, Donna, Toni Trent Parker, and Sheila Foster. *Black Books Galore! Guide to Great African American Children's Books.* New York: John Wiley & Sons, 1998.

Reid, Rob. *Family Storytime: Twenty-Four Creative Programs for All Ages.* Chicago: American Library Association, 1999.

Schimmel, Nancy. *Just Enough to Make a Story: A Sourcebook for Storytelling.* Berkeley, CA: Sisters' Choice, 1992.

Steele, Anitra T. *Bare Bones Children's Services: Tips for Public Library Generalists.* Chicago: American Library Association, 2001.

Stetson, Emily, and Vicky Congdon. *Little Hands Fingerplays and Action Songs: Seasonal Activities and Creative Play for 2- to 6-Year-Olds.* Charlotte, VT: Williamson Publishing, 2001.

Thomas, Rebecca L., and Catherine Barr. *Popular Series Fiction for K–6 Readers: A Reading and Selection Guide.* Westport, CT: Libraries Unlimited, 2005.

Various. *Intellectual Freedom for Children: The Censor Is Coming.* Chicago: American Library Association, 2000.

Various. *Unattended Children in the Public Library: A Resource Guide.* Chicago: American Library Association, 2002.

Walter, Virginia A. *Children & Libraries: Getting It Right.* Chicago: American Library Association, 2001.

Wolfman, Judy. *How and Why Stories for Readers Theatre.* Westport, CT: Libraries Unlimited, 2005.

Woolls, Blanche. *The School Library Media Manager.* 3d ed. Westport, CT: Libraries Unlimited, 2004.

Index

About the Author

PENNY PECK is Senior Librarian, Youth Services at the San Leandro Public Library in San Leandro, California.